Talcott Parsons

Actor, Situation and Normative Pattern

Studies in the Theory of Action

edited by

Prof. Dr. Helmut Staubmann (Universität Innsbruck)

and

Prof. Dr. Victor Lidz (Drexel University)

Volume 2

LIT

Talcott Parsons

Actor, Situation and Normative Pattern

An Essay in the Theory of Social Action

Edited by
Victor Lidz and Helmut Staubmann

LIT

Gedruckt mit Unterstützung des Bundesministeriums
für Wissenschaft und Forschung in Wien

Bibliographic information published by the Deutsche Nationalbibliothek
The Deutsche Nationalbibliothek lists this publication in the Deutsche Nationalbibliografie; detailed bibliographic data are available in the Internet at http://dnb.d-nb.de.

ISBN 978-3-8258-7500-8

A catalogue record for this book is available from the British Library

Krotenthallergasse 10/8
A-1080 Wien
Tel. +43 (0) 1-409 56 61
Fax +43 (0) 1-409 56 97
e-Mail: wien@lit-verlag.at
http://www.lit-verlag.at

LIT VERLAG Dr. W. Hopf
Berlin 2010
Fresnostr. 2
D-48159 Münster
Tel. +49 (0) 2 51-620 320
Fax +49 (0) 2 51-922 60 99
e-Mail: lit@lit-verlag.de
http://www.lit-verlag.de

Distribution:

In Germany: LIT Verlag Fresnostr. 2, D-48159 Münster
Tel. +49 (0) 2 51-620 32 22, Fax +49 (0) 2 51-922 60 99, e-mail: vertrieb@lit-verlag.de

In Austria: Medienlogistik Pichler-ÖBZ, e-mail: mlo@medien-logistik.at

In Switzerland: B + M Buch- und Medienvertrieb, e-mail: order@buch-medien.ch

In the UK: Global Book Marketing, e-mail: mo@centralbooks.com

In North America by:

Transaction Publishers
New Brunswick (U.S.A.) and London (U.K.)

Transaction Publishers
Rutgers University
35 Berrue Circle
Piscataway, NJ 08854

Phone: +1 (732) 445 - 2280
Fax: + 1 (732) 445 - 3138
for orders (U. S. only):
toll free (888) 999 - 6778
e-mail: orders@transactionpub.com

Contents

Preface

Victor Lidz

Shortly after Talcott Parsons' death in May of 1979, I began, as professional adviser to his estate, to collect his papers for transmission to the Harvard University Archives. Around the time of his formal retirement from Harvard in the spring of 1973, which precipitated his move to much smaller offices, Parsons had donated a substantial volume of his papers to the Archives, as he no longer had space in which to store them. After his death, however, the preponderance of his papers needed to be collected, identified, placed in some sort of order, and transmitted to the Archives. Current manuscripts and recent correspondence turned up in his study at home, in his office at Harvard, and in a file cabinet in the office of his secretary, Cathy Perkus. His older files of reprints, which were sent by a vast number of correspondents, turned up in file cabinets in a storage area of an unfinished floor of William James Hall at Harvard, where his offices had been for nearly fifteen years. Older manuscripts and teaching materials turned up in an old file cabinet and a bookcase in the basement of his home and, eventually, in the attic, where his wife, Helen Parsons, found the typescript for *The Structure of Social Action.*

Among the materials in the basement file cabinet was the long typescript, "Actor, Situation and Normative Pattern; An Essay in the Theory of Social Action." The document had clearly been Parsons' personal copy as it contained inserts to the text in his handwriting. Although I had been Parsons' undergraduate and graduate student, research assistant, protégé, and colleague for some nineteen years, I had never seen the document before, did not recall his ever having mentioned it, and had never noticed references to it in publications or other manuscripts. Upon reading it, I found it to be one of the most important manuscripts among the several that Parsons had left unpublished during his long career.

Study of the references to published works in the manuscript indicate that none of them appeared later than 1939. Moreover, the manuscript referred to Parsons' major work, *The Structure of Social Action* (New York: McGraw-Hill, 1937), as having been recently published. It, therefore, seemed likely that the work had been written or at least completed in 1939. Discussions with my fellow advisors to the Parsons estate, Harry M. Johnson and Jackson Toby, provided information about the manuscripts. Johnson, who had begun to study with Parsons before World War II, said that he was very familiar with the work. Starting no later, and possibly a little earlier than 1940, Parsons had distributed it to students as a current overview of the theory of action. Toby, who had studied with Parsons after World War II, reported that it had been distributed to students in the late 1940s, apparently down to the time when manuscript materials for *Toward A General Theory of Action* (Talcott Parsons and Edward A. Shils, editors: Cambridge, MA: Harvard University Press) and *The Social System* (Talcott Parsons: New York: Free Press, 1951) supplanted it. Thus, for ten or eleven years, the essay had been the chief sequel to *The Structure of Social Action,* acting as a technical source on Parsons' theory of social action.

It is thus a particular pleasure for me, as a student of the theory of action and its development, to see this landmark work published in English for the first time, approximately seventy years after it was written. It will help students of sociological theory to understand how Parsons developed the elaborate formulations of "Values, Motives, and Systems of Action," written with Edward A. Shils for *Toward A General Theory of Action,* and *The Social System* from the conceptual scheme presented in *The Structure of Social Action,* where Parsons deliberately limited himself to fundamental and general concepts. It thus partially addresses what many scholars have found to be one of the most intriguing mysteries in the development of Parsons' thought, namely, as to what were the intermediate developments in theory that led him from the very basic conceptual scheme of *The Structure of Social Action* to the far more elaborated schemas of "Values, Motives, and Systems of Action" and *The Social System.*

Readers will be pleased to find that in *Actor, Situation and Normative Pattern,* Parsons presents his ideas in a methodical manner, explaining key steps in the elaboration of the action frame of reference with greater clarity than in most of his later theoretical works. Not only does the long essay cover parts of the progression in Parsons' ideas that are not explained elsewhere, but it does so with a directness, specificity, and lucidity frequently missing from his later theoretical writings.

Actor, Situation and Normative Pattern was published previously in German in an edition prepared by Professor Harald Wenzel. I am indebted to Professor Helmut Staubmann for making the arrangements with LIT Verlag for the series of volumes on the theory of social action that we edit jointly, which has created the occasion for an English edition of Parsons' work. Professor Staubmann and I have tried to explain the importance of Parsons' essay in more detail in our collaborative introduction.

I thank Angela Eberhardt for her excellent work in typing the old manuscript into an electronic file for modern publication. In preparing the manuscript, we have used a carbon copy of the original typescript that Parsons apparently kept for his own use. It includes a number of handwritten corrections and marginal notes in Parsons' own handwriting. I have edited the manuscript lightly, changing few words, allowing many instances of Parsons' unusual grammatical constructions to stand, but altering punctuation for clarity in many places. I have left the pronoun "he" to stand for an individual actor, regardless of gender, in the standard usage of Parsons' time. The many partial references have been completed, but I have limited them to editions that were available to Parsons at the time of writing rather than inserting references to current or at least more recent editions. This is especially true of works of Max

Weber and Emile Durkheim, that were only available to Parsons in German and French. I thank the Harvard University Archives for permission to publish this work.

Introduction

Victor Lidz and Helmut Staubmann

Talcott Parsons' monograph, *Actor, Situation and Normative Pattern; An Essay in the Theory of Social Action,* though left unpublished in his lifetime, was his principal work of general theory between *The Structure of Social Action* of 1937 and the long essay, "Values, Motives, and Systems of Action," written with Edward A. Shils and published in *Toward A General Theory of Action* in 1951. *Actor, Situation and Normative Pattern* was apparently written or at least completed in 1939 and used in Parsons' teaching until around 1950, when manuscript materials for "Values, Motives, and Systems of Action" and *The Social System,* also published in 1951, became available for distribution to students and colleagues in the "purple prose" of "Dittoes" (a common method for producing multiple copies of a typescript before the Xerox machine was invented). Thus, the monograph stood for ten years or more as the standard current statement of the theory of social action in Parsons' teaching. Its status as a standard work for a decade in the evolution of Parsons' thought and teaching would, in itself, make the monograph an important document in the history of sociological theory well worthy of critical study.

The importance of the monograph goes beyond the merely historical, however. The work sheds important light on Parsons' distinctive way of theorizing as well as on the development of the theory of action over the course of his career. Thus, it adds substantially to our understanding of how his works should be construed and evaluated.

The development of Parsons' theory has often been interpreted as divided, depending on the phase of his career, in three discrete and more or less inconsistent frames of reference. The three frames of reference and phases of his thought are typically designated as: 1) the voluntarism of early essays and *The Structure of Social Action* (*SSA*), 2) a middle phase of "structural functionalism," a term that Parsons later explicitly disavowed, and 3) a late phase of pure functionalism. The pure functionalism is based on the four-function paradigm and the hypothesis that systems of action of any size or scope can fruitfully be analyzed in terms of four functional aspects, namely, adaptation, goal attainment, integration, and pattern maintenance. Parsons hypothesized in the mature pure functionalist phase that complex systems of action tend to differentiate into subsystems along the lines of the four functional dimensions.

In this common overview of the evolution of Parsons' thought, earlier conceptual schemes and theoretical formulations are often said simply to have been abandoned in favor of later ones, having little to do with their predecessors. *Actor, Situation and Normative Pattern*, however, reveals that there are important continuities across the phases of development in the theory of action. Although Parsons did, as he himself often said, "reserve the right to change his mind" on certain theoretical issues, the basic pattern of development in his theory was one of the further conceptual differentiation. He did not so much abandon earlier conceptual schemes as supplant them with more refined, complex, and detailed successors. The newer formulations generally do not render the older conceptual schemes invalid so much as integrate them within broader frames of reference and more specific sets of theoretical distinctions.

At the outset of *Actor, Situation and Normative Pattern,* Parsons states that the monograph represents a first effort to outline the frame of reference of the theory of action in abstraction from the effort to document, through the so-called convergence argument, its historical formation. He explicitly underscores a basic continuity with his previous work as well as conceptual innovation. In *SSA*, he had demonstrated a convergence among the conceptual schemes of several leading figures of the prior generation of social scientists, Alfred Marshall, Vilfredo Pareto, Emile Durkheim, and Max Weber. To establish the convergence, he had deliberately limited his presentation of the theory of action to a statement of basic and essential elements that he could show had been incorporated into the theories of all four of his great predecessors. *SSA* was not written as a treatise in the intellectual history of social science in the several decades before the start of Parsons' own career, as it has often been treated in secondary literature. Rather, it was a demonstration of the necessity of retaining each of the basic and essential elements (or their logical and empirical equivalents) in any frame of reference designed for the analysis of social action. In *Actor, Situation and Normative Pattern,* Parsons returns to the same basic frame of reference, but undertakes what became his lifelong task of elaborating that frame of reference toward a general theory for guiding research across empirical domains within the social sciences. While the argument of *Actor, Situation and Normative Pattern* still proceeds at a high level of generality, Parsons introduces a number of conceptual innovations not present in *SSA* or in his pre-*SSA* essays. Moreover, he does so in terms that anticipate some of the key arguments through which he would add further specificity in the works published in 1951. Indeed, the discussions in "Values, Motives, and Systems of Action" and *The Social System* build in basic ways on ideas first developed in *Actor, Situation and Normative Pattern.* However, Parsons justified some basic steps in the conceptual development of the theory of action with a directness and clarity in *Actor, Situation and Normative Pattern* that he either did not repeat or reprised less thoroughly in later works. It is for this reason that we, as editors, present the monograph as an important aid to a comprehensive understanding of the development of the theory of action, even in its later forms.

In *SSA*, Parsons formulated the frame of reference for the theory of social action with a focus on the abstract and general entity of the "unit act," a minimal instance of meaningful human conduct on the part of an individual actor. He argued that in all cases, a unit act is possible only through the conjunction of ends, means, norms, and the conditions within which action takes place. In some formulations, he added an element of the effort that an actor must expend to implement a unit act. Parsons' starting point had been Max Weber's statement to the effect that all human conduct involves ends and means, implying that ends and means are universal and, hence, fundamental categories for the analysis of action. Action can never be understood or analyzed without reference to the categories of ends and means. Parsons extended Weber's claim by adding that norms regulating conduct are similarly universal because action cannot be sustained within and across social relationships unless there are rules that the parties can rely upon to constrain one another's choices of ends and means. Norms are thus irreducible, given the social nature of human action or conduct. Similarly, action always takes place within a setting in which there are conditions that cannot all be mobilized as means to be used to attain ends. The distinction between means and conditions thus rests on what in the setting or environment is utilized as an instrument for attaining an end or goal and what remains external to the particular course of action, yet imposes a limitation or constraint on it.

Among the elements of the unit act, Parsons placed the greatest emphasis on norms. In part, this was because norms comprise the element that was excluded from the frame of reference of utilitarian thought, the most widely accepted conceptual scheme in the social sciences at the time that Parsons was writing. Parsons highlighted the respects in which norms are essential to the action frame of reference precisely because he wished to demonstrate the inadequacy of utilitarian thought. In particular, he emphasized that utilitarian thought, with its exclusion of the category of norms, is incapable of resolving what he called the "problem of order" – that is, of explaining how societies and other social systems have the capacity for ordering social interaction – without invoking such *ad hoc* explanations as the Leviathan in Hobbes' theory or the "natural harmony of interests" in Locke's or Adam Smith's theories. In the background, Parsons argued that the element of norm represents at the level of the unit act what at the level of whole communities or entire societies are very extensive normative structures, a vast empirical reality to which utilitarian theories tended (and still tend) to be blind. In *SSA*, Parsons also underscored the importance of general conceptions of value, including their premises in religious belief systems, that Max Weber and Emile Durkheim had both demonstrated to be central to normative orders.

These formulations from *SSA* comprised the point of departure for the conceptual innovations of *Actor, Situation and Normative Pattern.* Parsons believed that his previous work had established them as essential to any future theory of social action, but he also acknowledged that they were far too elementary to serve as a sufficient scheme for orienting future empirical research. In his new monograph, he introduced four key theoretical innovations and sought to explore the intricate interconnections among them.

The innovations of *Actor, Situation and Normative Pattern* rest on a methodology, previously articulated in *SSA,* that emphasizes the importance of frame of reference or conceptual scheme. Following the methodology of science propounded by senior figures at Harvard University, especially Alfred North Whitehead, Lawrence J. Henderson, and James B. Conant, Parsons underscored in all his works that intellectual disciplines, including sociology, must develop coherent sets of concepts to guide their modalities of abstracting empirical facts and generalizations from the observable external world. In the terms of this methodology, a conceptual scheme is *logically* prior to statements of facts and empirical generalizations in any science or intellectual discipline. Even if a conceptual scheme has been revised in the light of prior empirical discoveries, as often occurs, its logical function of establishing modalities of abstraction remains basic. Parsons often quoted Henderson to the effect that facts are not the phenomena of the external world but statements about such phenomena. As statements, they require concepts. To synthesize complex bodies of facts in coherent ways, a discipline requires a set of logically integrated concepts – what Whitehead termed a frame of reference. Although Parsons' writings include many factual observations and generalizations, empirical hypotheses, and abstract general theorems, his major works focus on the logically prior task of establishing frames of reference for fruitful social scientific abstraction from the phenomenal world. Parsons regarded methodical critique of possible conceptual schemes and then synthesis of a unifying, comprehensive frame of reference as his key contribution to social science. It was a task to which he returned repeatedly in the course of his career, and eventually he formulated the theory of action in terms of a hierarchy of multiple frames of reference for synthesizing different levels and aspects of social scientific knowledge.

Parsons understood that synthesizing a frame of reference or set of frames of reference is a *preliminary* though essential phase of the research enterprise. It was meant to facilitate empirical research, guiding specific investigations to fruitful findings and ones that can be integrated with findings of other investigations. The focus on frames of reference was not intended to produce a completed body of knowledge or general synthesis of a discipline without extensive independent and more specialized empirical research. In his concentration on formulating basic frames of reference, Parsons' understanding of how to develop sociological thought was very different from that of the classical "Grand Theorists," such as, Comte or Spencer, even though he has at times been grouped with them. He well understood that frames of reference are, in logical form, very different from empirical results of research, as necessary as they are to empirical investigation. The key innovations of *Actor, Situation and Normative Pattern* are refinements and extensions of the frame of reference first introduced in *SSA*.

The first of the four basic innovations is signaled in the very title of the monograph. Parsons shifted the focus of his frame of reference from the unit act to the actor engaged in a social *situation*. He suggested that the actor's relation to the situation is parallel to the organism's relation to the environment in biological theory, and equally fundamental. Just as the organism's relation to the environment created a dynamic focus for evolutionary theory in biology, so a concentration on the actor's relation to the situation should open up a new potential for dynamic theorizing in sociology. Parsons proposed that the meaningful orientation of the actor to the situation is what distinguishes it from the same individual's relation as a biological organism to the environment. The distinction is analytical, with the meaningful orientation of the actor indexing an emergent level of relations or systems independent of the biological level. Empirically, the two levels may be profoundly intertwined, but the level of meaningful orientation is intrinsically independent of biological processes of adaptation.

The focus on the actor's relation to the situation immediately brings other actors into the picture. Situations typically involve some plurality of actors. The actor engaged in a situation generally has reciprocal relationships with another actor or actors, perhaps many other actors. His or her meaningful orientation to the situation entails orientations to other actors who, in turn, are meaningfully oriented to him or her. Actors are parts of the situation for one another and thus objects to one another's orientations and conduct. Each actor is both a subject with meaningful orientations to the others and an object of the intentions and actions of the others. Parsons quickly concludes that conformity with the expectations and standards of conduct that the various participants in a situation communicate to one another is intrinsically problematic. This conclusion is simply a reformulation of the problem of order highlighted in *SSA,* but it now grounds Parsons' argument, later on elaborated in *The Social System,* that social control is a universal of social process. In every situation in which social interaction takes place, there is a risk of deviance on the part of some or all actors with respect to the expectations of other actors. Thus, there is always a need for mechanisms of social control. This is an issue to which Parsons returns later in the monograph.

The second of Parsons' major innovations concerns the actor's meaningful orientation to the situation. Parsons suggested that there are three general categories of orientation: *cognitive, affective,* and what he called *teleological.* Each of the three categories draws upon very extensive bodies of common culture as background to how particular actors orient themselves to the immediate situations they encounter. But each of the three categories of orientation is also involved in the creative ways that a voluntaristic actor engages situations and manages to orient his or her conduct within those situations.

An orientation is cognitive insofar as it is concerned with knowing or understanding objects in the situation. A cognitive orientation may be concerned with everyday knowledge of objects and how to relate to them – the sort of simply practical understanding that Alfred Schutz termed *recipe knowledge,* such as, how to drive a car, tune a television to favorite channels, or write a check to pay for purchases. Or, it may involve the highly disciplined knowledge that is found in the sciences, as in an astrophysicists' knowledge of distant galaxies or economists' knowledge of how prices change when goods become more or less scarce. Actors typically command a vast range of cognitive information that they use to orient themselves to the situations and environments in which they conduct their lives, and for most of them various mixtures of everyday, magical, and highly disciplined forms of understanding are involved. A distinctive quality of modern civilization, however, is the degree to which the sphere of magical belief has become restricted and highly disciplined knowledge has gained predominance in the form of the sciences. To be sure, relatively small proportions of the population are qualified scientists, but scientifically validated knowledge has gained great prestige; its implications are widely accepted even by lay people who lack expert understanding of science, and it is available to orient the teaching, research, and efforts to solve practical problems of the minority who are scientists.

An orientation is affective insofar as it concerns the feeling-states or emotions of the actor. Affective orientations relate to the actual or anticipated pleasure of action. Parsons acknowledges that affects or states of pleasure and unpleasure often arise within an individual's biological organism and, thus, may originate outside the action frame of reference.

However, they enter the process of action and become affective states of the actor when the feelings of pleasure or unpleasure are combined with affective orientations, typically culturally patterned orientations. The pleasure gained from listening to the music of Bach, Mozart, or Beethoven is not derived entirely from the physics of the sounds or the biology of hearing, but depends on engagement in a cultural tradition of appreciation. Our appreciation of a fine meal follows not merely a process of digestion, but more importantly the appreciative traditions of a cuisine. When we are emotionally moved by viewing a fine painting, the biology of our vision is merely a condition of a cultivated act of appreciating art. Parsons held that we encounter many of the persons and material objects in our daily lives through affective orientations that are often based on intensely personal experience as well as being shaped by long-standing cultural traditions. With regard to the meaning of social objects – other persons – he cites Freud's writings on transference as demonstrating how affective attitudes toward parents, teachers, and other important figures in our early lives may shape feelings toward others. He also notes the complex affective meanings that individuals in modern societies hold toward objects of prestige and status symbols.

An orientation is teleological insofar as it is forward-looking in the conduct of an actor and provides a guide to future courses of action. Teleological orientations enable the actor to make choices of ends and means and relate them to normative principles and standards regulating conduct in the applicable situation. They are, Parsons says, imperative in mood, giving orders to the actor, and thereby contrasting with the indicative mood of cognitive orientations and with the affective interests of the actor. Teleological orientations are concerned, above all, with the moral and normative guidance of the actor in planning his or her conduct. They draw upon the moral culture of the society and provide standards of conduct that are typically shared by the actors involved in a situation together. As Parsons later makes clear, the institutionalization of moral culture as the normative order of a social system, the basis for the sharing of moral orientations among individual participants in the social system, establishes the core of its normative order, its particular solution to the Hobbesian problem of social order. In this respect, the teleological is the most salient category of orientations for sociological analysis. Parsons' emphasis on teleological orientations draws together, in greater depth than his discussions in *SSA,* the voluntaristic frame of reference focusing on the ultimately independent choices of actors, on the one hand, and the approach to solving the problem of order by emphasizing shared and constraining normative standards of conduct, on the other hand. His discussion of the teleologic decision-making of the actor is somewhat more complex than his treatment of the actor's moral orientation, the term he later substituted for teleological orientation, in "Values, Motives and Systems of Action" and in *The Social System.* In the publications of 1951, moral orientations continue to hold the center stage for sociological analysis, but other elements of the teleological category, such as, selection of ends and means, are treated as part of the on-going voluntaristic process of social action.

Parsons quickly noted that, within social situations, not only does the actor of initial reference hold cognitive, affective, and teleological orientations, but so does each of the other actors involved. Social objects within a situation are themselves actors and, hence, they respond to the actor of reference in terms of their own orientations. In earlier formulations of his later emphasis on the "double contingency" of interaction, Parsons notes that all social action involves at least a double relation: how a given actor affects the courses of action of others and how their courses of action affect him or her. Each actor thus necessarily develops orientations to the situation to assess it cognitively, affectively, and teleologically or morally. A sequence of social action is in part an open dialogue among the complex, multi-dimensional orientations maintained by the various actors, whether parents and children, professional colleagues in different fields of specialization, employer and employees, or political leaders and followers. Moreover, actors are also objects to one another, and thus they typically have cognitive, affective, and teleological meanings as objects of one another's conduct. To be a parent, colleague, employer, or political leader to others is to hold specific cognitive, affective, and teleological significance for them. Parsons' discussion probes at some length, first, the ways in which cognitive, affective, and teleological orientations, while remaining empirically independent of one another, also enter into various forms of combination and, second, the ways in which actors' orientations relate to the cognitive, affective, and teleological significance of the social objects or other actors encountered in social situations. For example, the attitudes of moral respect and its opposite, moral indignation, involve complex linkages between affective and normative-teleological orientations toward a social or cultural object, such as, a teacher or a work of philosophy. Parsons proposes that three sets of antithetical complex orientations, pleasure and pain, moral respect and indignation, and love and hate, though empirically as well as conceptually independent, tend to move into affective alignment with one another in the motivations of actors. Objects that give pleasure tend also to be respected and loved, and objects that cause pain are generally viewed with indignation and even hate. However, Parsons does not posit that the pleasure versus pain orientation is primary in a causal sense. The moral indignation projected toward a political figure, for example, may give rise to hate and even feelings of pain in reaction to his or her policies.

Large sections of *Actor, Situation and Normative Pattern* are devoted to analyzing social situations, in terms of the give-and-take between the three-dimensional orientations of actors and the complementary three-dimensional meanings of social objects. The discussion is wide-ranging and perhaps the most original in the monograph. Much of it proceeds under the influence of Max Weber and his treatment of rational action as an ideal type from which actors in various situations may deviate in specific ways, whether through the intrusion of irrational affect, the predominance of magical components in a tradition of cognitive orientation, or the simple absence of intellectually disciplined cognition. Following up his analysis in *SSA,* Parsons argues that "rational" choices of ends as well as means are formed in terms of broader orientational standards, such as advancing economic production or economic efficiency. He similarly argues that allocation of means among alternative or competing ends cannot be accomplished on sheerly cognitive bases, but requires reference to standards for setting priorities, including relative emphasis on economic, political, familial, or other domains of action. He notes that economic production, even under the most favorable and efficient technological conditions, necessarily entails the sacrifice of foregone opportunities to pursue other ends and other uses of means and thus cannot be maintained without normative standards to justify the choices made. The analysis of rational action and its necessary dependence, in many respects, upon a broad normative order also represents Parsons' effort to establish parametric limits to the validity of the post-Marshallian neo-liberal economics that was rapidly gaining the status of an orthodoxy at the time he wrote. His discussion represents the most technical and detailed of his engagements with economic theory down to *Economy and Society,* written with Neil J. Smelser and published in 1956.

Other sections of the discussion of orientations in relation to social situations are heavily influenced by Sigmund Freud, the first of Parsons' writings to be so influenced. Parsons insists that affective attitudes enter into all decision-making processes. He thus highlights the affective aspects of the basic elements of action: ends and even means are typically chosen because of their connections to the affective interests of actors; the sense of obligation to observe normative patterns is bound up with affective attachments to them. The intensity of an individual's affective attachment to ends provides the basic motive for expending effort in the course of any action. Any "system of moral values" must be supported by appropriate affective attitudes, including, in particular, the attitude of moral respect for key values and that of moral indignation for antithetical values. In a significant extension of Freud, Parsons proposed that the theory of normative order, in general, must address the phenomena of psychological introjection of moral and normative orientations and their integration with the general affective and motivational orientations of individuals. This proposal clearly derives from Freud's conception of the superego, but also a Durkheimian perspective on the coherence of a complicated collective conscience or normative order.

The third of the basic innovations presented in *Actor, Situation and Normative Pattern* extends Parsons' analysis of the complexity of actors' orientations to one another to examine how they interact within shared social situations. Parsons explored the processes of interaction in terms of an elementary model of a relationship between two actors, A and B. However, the model acknowledged that each actor's orientation, with its cognitive, affective, and teleological elements, as well as his or her ends and means are independent of, although also interdependent with, the other's. Actor B thus has a variety of capacities to assist Actor A in efforts to attain his or her goals. But B equally commands capacities to try to frustrate A's pursuit of his or her goals. Parsons focuses on the tactics and mechanisms that each of the actors can use to affect the conduct of the other.

Perhaps the most general tactic is to offer rewards or punishments contingent on the other's course of action. Actor A may promise Actor B a positive sanction or reward if B acts in a manner that accords with A's expectations. The sanction need not be material; it can consist of pleasure, love, respect, recognition, esteem, and so forth. However, there are obvious costs to this tactic: how much reward must be promised to assure B's compliance? Can A always afford the costs, whether material or affectual? Instead, A may simply inform B that a negative sanction or punishment will be imposed if B acts in a way that frustrates A's efforts. This tactic may deter B from obstructing A's planned course of action and may be the more direct and cost-free method of securing A's end, assuming that A can attain his or her end without more positive cooperation from B. However, if B actually acts to obstruct A's efforts, then A must impose the punishment or suffer a loss of credibility with B and perhaps other actors in the situation. Again, the punishment need not be material, but may consist in displeasure, withdrawal or love, affection, recognition, esteem, and so forth. Of course, it is in the logic of the interactive model of their relationship that B may simultaneously be seeking to sanction A by offering rewards, threatening punishments, or actually imposing punishments. In particular, such negative sanctions as the imposition of displeasure or withdrawal of love by A are likely, then, to be reciprocated by B and may be painful to A. The course of interaction can never be apprehended by viewing the tactics of sanctioning from the perspective of only A or B.

Parsons perceives other possibilities in the interaction as well. Actor A can attempt to "persuade" B to act in accord with A's expectations on the grounds of shared interests, sympathies, duties, or solidarity. It may be possible, in this way, to obtain B's cooperation in a course of conduct without having to absorb the costs of extending a reward or the disruptions to the relationship of imposing – or even threatening – a negative sanction. Parsons notes that persuasion can take the form of appeal to the interests of the other as a rational actor, of appeal to value principles shared between or among actors, or various combinations of the two. It is in the logic of persuasion, however, that its use, and the invoking of solidarity as a ground of cooperation, leaves A open to B's later invoking the solidary relationship in a reciprocal request for help. The obligation that is created may thus create a later cost. Parsons also notes that either A or B, often in the process of persuasion, may withhold information from or provide false information to the other in order to gain his or her cooperation by fraud. Modern commercial advertising and, in particular, political propaganda may draw on characteristics of both the pure type of persuasion and the pure type of fraud. Parsons observed that Actor A or Actor B may also seek to compel compliance from the other by forcing changes in the situation of the other without the other's choice. Arresting or imprisoning an individual is compulsion in this sense. In emphasizing the sociological importance of fraud and force, Parsons, as in *SSA,* is acknowledging the empirical importance of Hobbesian solutions to the problem of order, unsatisfactory as they may be as a ground for general sociological theory.

The reciprocal sanctioning practices of actors engaged in a common situation gain stability, Parsons suggests, in the integration of the actors' affective attitudes with the moral-normative elements of their teleological orientations. Their sanctioning practices reflect the reciprocal nature of social interaction, but also a mutual reliance on teleological orientations that ultimately include basic value-principles. The exchange of sanctions through interaction constitutes processes of social control because the participating actors in a given social system are typically oriented to consistent value principles. This is a theme to which Parsons returned at various times and in various theoretical contexts later in his career – notably in the chapter, "Deviance and Social Control," in *The Social System* and, to rather different theoretical ends, in his famous papers, "On the Concept of Political Power" and "On the Concept of Influence," both reprinted in his collection of essays, *Politics and Social Structure.*

Although the discussion of sanctioning practices and social control proceeds mainly at the level of actors considered in abstraction from particular empirical situations, Parsons does not presume that the actors are necessarily equals. In offering rewards or threatening punishments, Actor A may have a position of authority over Actor B, for examples, as boss or manager in a corporation. The individual seeking to persuade another may also have a prestigious status, perhaps as a political leader hoping to gain support, as a resource for invoking a solidary relationship. A person exercising compulsion over another typically has the powers of a public office – for example, as police officer or judge – as a ground of his or her capacity to act. Thus, the analysis of sanctioning practices has in the background a need to analyze the statuses and hierarchies associated with social institutions. This leads us to the fourth of the innovations that Parsons introduces into the action frame of reference in *Actor, Situation and Normative Pattern,* namely, analysis of stabilization and structuralization, a term he used sparingly in later works, of social relationships.

It is in this fourth context that Parsons introduces, as related, the concepts of social system, homeostasis, and function for this first time in his career. Given their future importance in the body of his work, it is apparent that this innovation – or set of innovations – signals a major step in the evolution of his thought. Homeostasis is a concept that W. B. Cannon introduced in his book on physiology, *The Wisdom of the Body.* It refers to a capacity of complex systems to maintain an overall stability in its internal processes by responding to any perturbing effects with countervailing forces, as when an organism responds to heat by sweating to keep its temperature within "normal" limits, becomes thirsty and drinks more liquid when its blood thickens slightly, or produces more insulin when the level of sugar in the blood rises. For Parsons, an attractive feature of Cannon's account of homeostasis was that it involves equilibria or balances among many complexly interacting forces within an organism. Human societies, too, might be understood as maintaining highly complex balances among a great many differentiated forces or energies. Parsons thought that perhaps his model of interaction among independent-but-interdependent actors provided a rudimentary understanding of how potentially opposing or countervailing social forces can be brought into balances. However, a true overview of a social or societal homeostasis would require an analysis of the differentiation of forces or energies within a system. In his discussion of the stabilization of social systems, he sought to begin such an analysis of differentiation. The discussion proceeds at several levels.

At the first level, he continues the discussion of interaction and social control by placing it in the context of an ongoing social system. He thus suggests that actors must have ways of disapproving and delimiting antisocial conduct and other conduct that may tend to detract from a positive integration of the social system. He then argues that it is by maintaining common moral or normative standards that a social system gains the "selective mechanisms" to favor strategies and tactics of interaction that support integrative over disintegrative forces. Moreover, the common moral standards must be internalized within the affective orientations of individual actors, so that they will hold sentiments of moral attachment to a normative order. Such sentiments will lead actors to react with moral indignation whenever another person's conduct challenges the normative order. Similarly, they will lead to inhibitory feelings of guilt on the part of actors who themselves develop motives to act contrary to normative expectations. Insofar as a normative order is maintained in these ways, actors will oppose perturbing conduct on the part of others with direct and effective tactics of interaction, whether providing positive or negative material sanctions, persuasion, or even compulsion. That is, the relationships of interaction will exercise social control over deviant tendencies, and the social system made up of such relationships will maintain integration or homeostasis. This analysis, again, presents the core of an argument concerning social control that Parsons later developed in considerably greater detail in *The Social System.*

Parsons then proceeds to emphasize further the importance of common values and their internalization by another line of argument and by considering another aspect of social organization. Individual members of a society contribute to it in a variety of social roles. In modern societies, chief among these roles are occupational roles, although members of society make contributions to the community in many other types of roles as well – as parents, as members of voluntary associations, as participants in politics, and so forth. Societies necessarily have ways of ranking the social contributions made by individuals in their various roles, especially their occupational roles. Parsons says that there is an "intrinsically quantitative" aspect of these rankings, where some roles and contributions are more highly valued and ranked than others. Were there not general agreement in a community on the overall relative rankings of social roles – and such dimensions of ranking as achievement, wealth, authority, and "birth" or family connection – members of the society would not likely feel motivated to fulfill the expectations of the more demanding roles. Thus, common value principles and the sentiments attached to them are essential to the status order or system of stratification in communities and societies. The integration of the society would not be possible without shared evaluative principles for social stratification and without affective attachment to the value principles on the part of members of the community.

Parsons acknowledges that different occupational roles are founded on somewhat different normative principles and standards. The creativity valued in an artist is different from that valued in the entrepreneur and the scientist. The physician and the teacher have fiduciary obligations to their patients and students that the business person does not have to customers. The superb physical coordination of the professional athlete is not so necessary for the insurance salesman, nor for the specialist in internal medicine, but quite possibly for the neurosurgeon. The originality of the advertising copy writer is different from that of the scholar. There can be no question but that each calling rests on its own values and norms for assessing the quality and importance of the contributions of role incumbents. However, Parsons argues, these various sets of specific evaluative complexes must integrate with one another under more highly generalized value-principles. Only then can the many kinds of contributions made by the many members of a society be integrated with one another into a homeostatic system.

Notably, it is in the context of analyzing mechanisms of integration that Parsons first uses the terms function and functional necessity. In *Actor, Situation, and Normative Pattern,* the concept of function of a social system is limited to its integration; that is, functional analysis concerns only the integrative qualities of a system with diverse and potentially conflicting components. However, Parsons clearly articulates the broader concept of the need of a system for a specific quality of homeostatic relationships among its parts. In *The Social System,* he expanded, essentially, the same conception of function to include allocation of means or resources among the units of a society as well as integration among its units. Later, he developed the famous four-function paradigm emphasizing the independent functional relationships involved in adaptation, goal attainment, integration, and pattern maintenance. Of the four, adaptation and integration were presented in terms quite similar to the two functions acknowledged in *The Social System.*

By comparison to the later treatments, the discussion of function in *Actor, Situation and Normative Pattern* was quite limited. Yet, it opened a crucial topic for further exploration.

Although the idea of function did not figure significantly in the argument of *SSA* – there is no index entry for it – institution played a central part. Thus, expansion of the action frame of reference required reexamination of the concept of institution. In *Actor, Situation and Normative Pattern*, Parsons distinguished four elements of social institutions. First, institutions regulate statuses and the relationships among them. For example, the institution of the market regulates the statuses of buyer and seller and that of the university regulates the statuses of professor and student and of undergraduate and graduate student. Second, institutions define the legitimate expectations associated with the various regulated statuses. The institution of employment defines what employers may normatively expect of their employees (types and rates of work, but not typically qualities of family life) and employees of their employers (pay, safe work conditions, freedom from harassment, but not control of the corporation). Third, institutional relationships are supported by social sanctions. In the institution of a business corporation, for example, capital funds enable the management to make payments in exchange for supplies of raw materials and to compensate employees, while managers in positions of authority have the capacity to sanction other members of the staff if they fail to fulfill expectations, perhaps by reducing their pay or even firing them. Fourth, institutions become part of the social structure by virtue of being generally recognized by members of the society. Institutions, such as, contract, property, incorporation, employment, and the market, in modern societies have become elements of the social order that are ordinarily taken utterly for granted as frames for everyday relationships.

Parsons then gives particular attention to two basic types of modern institutions. Formal organization involves rational organization of human services, generally focused on a specific domain of activity. Administrative bureaus of governments, business corporations, and universities are all examples of formal organization. They all involve social roles and statuses set apart from the "personal" spheres of members. Formal organization generally involves relationships of authority among members who perform different roles and hold different statuses. Typically authority relations are hierarchical, but also bounded, with different branches of an organization being regulated by different authorities. Authority may also be structured collegially, as when members of a committee must act collectively or by majority vote for their decisions to take effect. Authority is also bounded in that typically it does not bind individuals who have no role in the organization. However, authority relations in formal organizations are generally supported by coercive sanctions. To be sure, authoritative decisions do not typically require coercion to take effect. In most organizations, the objects of directives from higher officials simply observe legitimate directives – that is, follow orders that appear legal and morally proper. Yet, if individuals bound by a directive decide not to observe it, the authorities may resort to coercion to enforce their decisions.

Law is the other formal institution to which Parsons attends. He begins by addressing the complex issue of when a normative order should be considered law, and takes a different position than he would late in his career. He specifies that law exists only when the administration of a normative pattern becomes the specialized function of a governing authority. It is a definition that emphasizes a close interdependence between law and formal organization. Parsons then highlights three elements of the formal administration of law. First is the formal interpretation of normative patterns, a key aspect of the judicial function. Second is the adjudication of disputes, typically by a formally impartial party, such as, a court, arbitrator, or mediator. Third is enforcement of the normative patterns, as in the order of a judge in deciding a civil suit, perhaps finding that one party must pay damages to the other party, or in imposing a fine or sentence on a guilty party in a criminal case. None of these characteristics of the law can exist in the absence of a formally organized public authority and specifically a court system. The law in

Parsons' sense is thus an essential aspect of the formal rationalization, in Weber's sense, of normative patterns. Such formal rationality tends, over time, to penetrate many spheres of the normative order of a society and practically all other social institutions.

Parsons concludes *Actor, Situation and Normative Pattern* by stressing again that his intent has been to formulate the action frame of reference in more differentiated terms, ones that are closer to giving practical guidance for social scientific research. He also emphasizes that he has not attempted to create a closed system of theory. The action frame of reference is an open body of theory, subject to continuing conceptual development, reformulation, and refinement. This methodological stance is one to which Parsons adhered throughout his career. It contrasts sharply with interpretations by those who have viewed the theory of action as a closed system.

There are interesting elements of the discussion in *Actor, Situation and Normative Pattern* that the present discussion, with its focus on four general theoretical innovations, has had to bypass, yet which the reader should appreciate. One is that Parsons introduces materials from anthropology and then-current psychoanalytic thought in ways that have previously been in the published record only from the late 1940s and early 1950s. He devotes considerable discussion to the place of magic in orientations to action and to its relation, on the one hand, to religion and, on the other hand, to philosophically grounded cognition and science. Parsons acknowledges that all societies and cultures contain elements of rational cognitive knowledge by which actors can orient themselves to practical conditions within their environments and social situations. Yet, philosophically rationalized cognitive knowledge, and science, in particular, has received an entirely different order of cultivation in the modern West than in other cultures and civilizations. Parsons also retains Max Weber's attention to the importance of "problems of meaning" as aspects of human experience and potential sources of cultural and social change. He emphasizes that problems of meaning are, most likely, to emerge where established moral principles, especially ones articulated in religious belief system, are frustrated. Material and moral or spiritual suffering, the loss of love in personal life, and the experience of injustice or evil lead to problems of meaning in this sense for actors individually and, in some circumstances, collectively, with potentially broad social consequences.

Conclusion

Many critics have suggested that the years between *SSA* and *The Social System* were a fallow period in Parsons' career. Although he published a substantial number of essays, the record of writings published in this period does not include significant innovations in basic theory. Yet, other critics have perceived the conceptual scheme of *The Social System* as so radically different from that of *SSA* that they have wondered how and on what grounds Parsons arrived at the ideas around which the later work was organized. *Actor, Situation and Normative Pattern* shows that already in the first years of the period between 1937 and 1951, Parsons had developed significant conceptual and theoretical innovations. It also documents key steps along the conceptual path that Parsons took between *SSA* and his early essays, on the one hand, and "Values, Motives and Systems of Action" and *The Social System,* on the other hand.

By the time *Actor, Situation and Normative Pattern* was drafted, Parsons had already studied Freud with notable care and creative critical thought. He had then come to emphasize emotional-affective-motivational elements of action far more strongly than in his earlier writings and to integrate them within the general action frame of reference. Moreover, the monograph shows the first indications that Parsons intended to treat personality systems as independent of social institutions or systems and, yet, as in dynamic interconnection with them. What Parsons came to consider as a lack of anthropological thinking in his early work led – in a fashion parallel to his integration of psychoanalytic thought – to an emphasis on the importance of cultural dimensions of social action. The cultural emphasis is clearly adumbrated in *Actor, Situation and Normative Pattern,* although it is only in the works of 1951 that culture is presented as an independent subsystem of action coordinate with social and personality systems. Thus, we do not yet find in *Actor, Situation and Normative Pattern* the forthright distinctions among cultural, social, and personality systems as subsystems of action that became key innovations of T*oward A General Theory of Action* and T*he Social System.* Yet, we do find Parsons introducing considerations that led him later to those landmark formulations. In seeing the intermediate conceptual scheme, breaking out of the unitary formulations of the action frame of reference *SSA* and emphasizing the independence of cognitive, affective, and teleological elements of orientation, but not yet venturing the categorical distinctions among subsystems of action as in the 1951 publications, we can grasp the important continuities between the early and middle phases of Parsons' conceptual development.

The discussion of the structuralization of the social system in *Actor, Situation and Normative Pattern,* though in key respects fragmentary, nevertheless foreshadows much of value in Parsons' writings. It begins the development of a more explicit and penetrating analysis of social institutions than either Weber or Durkheim achieved. It initiates the analysis of role, status, and social stratification that Parsons was to elaborate in several later essays. It also made a fruitful start on the theory of structural differentiation among major spheres of society, an element of the theory of action which was to evolve into the analysis of subsystems of society after the four-function paradigm emerged in the mid-1950s. The treatment of reciprocal sanctioning relationships among actors later developed into the so-called "sanction paradigm," a key component of Parsons' theory of generalized media of interchange. In his analyses of sanctioning relationships, social control, authority, influence, and the role of value-attitudes in communication in the present monograph, Parsons already introduces specific themes that reappear repeatedly in essays of the 1950s and 1960s that led up to and then introduced the notion of generalized symbolic media.

Parsons' efforts to integrate anthropological and psychological theories into a sociologically centered framework for the analysis of human action are only two examples of a more general characteristic of Parsons' work, namely, its goal of broad interdisciplinary synthesis. Other key components of this synthesis include the adaptation of philosophical premises, in particular those of Whitehead's analytic realism, as a grounding for social scientific methodology; the adoption of key developments in biology and physiology, such as, the concept of homeostasis and general systems theory; and later, Norbert Wiener's idea of cybernetic relations among components of complex systems. The fundamental figure of actor and situation as expressed in the title of the present essay and described in its first section, conceived as parallel to organism and environment, follows basic ideas in the theory of evolution. Contrary to some other approaches to interdisciplinary theory in the social sciences, both in his time and in ours, Parsons sought further differentiation of his basic frame of reference, both internally and in relation to biology, in order to avoid reductionism. In this endeavor to achieve synthesis through a unified but multidimensional framework for the study of human action, there is a direct path from *Actor, Situation and Normative Pattern* to Parsons' last major essay, "The Paradigm of the Human Condition."

It remains unclear why Parsons did not publish a work as ambitious and fundamental as *Actor, Situation and Normative Pattern*. Possibly the reason is that the work is somewhat awkward in length – too long to place in a journal, but perhaps, in his estimation, it was too short for an independent volume. It is also possible that he continued to think of its formulations as provisional, and, hence, reserved publication for a work he could present as more definitive. When he published *Essays in Sociological Theory; Pure and Applied* in 1949, he did not include any essay nearly as long as *Actor, Situation and Normative Pattern*. Although a few of the essays in the volume addressed matters of comparable generality, *Actor, Situation and Normative Pattern* was not cited in discussions of their background. Parsons may have regarded the monograph as what he later termed a "working paper" to be followed up by writings more extensive, more detailed, and with conceptual revisions. We do know that, from early in the 1940s, shortly after completion of *Actor,*

Situation and Normative Pattern, Parsons had already started on a draft of a volume to which he gave the title, *The Social System.* His early draft chapters, although they attempt a more extended explication, are not as conceptually dense as *Actor, Situation and Normative Pattern.* Nor for the most part do they advance the basic elements of theory of action beyond, or even so far as, *Actor, Situation and Normative Pattern.* Parsons later discarded or radically revised and expanded the early draft materials before *The Social System* saw publication nearly a decade later. Thus, it is possible that *Actor, Situation and Normative Pattern,* whether from the time of its writing or soon thereafter, was for Parsons a sort of intensive stock-taking of basic ideas that he already planned to present in expanded and perhaps revised form in a larger-scale work.

The importance of *Actor, Situation and Normative Pattern* goes beyond its value as the original source of some of the concepts and analyses that Parsons first published in the works of 1951. In the essay of 1939, Parsons justified key steps in the conceptual development of the theory of action, including the presentation of arguments that he did not repeat or only sketched in lesser detail in subsequent works. A number of other points were discussed with a clarity that was not matched in later statements. Thus, the work continues to stand as an essential contribution to a comprehensive understanding of the theory of action, even in its later forms.

Our motives in publishing this important manuscript over seventy years after it was drafted are twofold. For scholars who are specialists in Parsons' theory of action, it contributes to understanding of the development of his body of thought. Moreover, it substantiates the long contested interpretation that emphasizes continuity rather than abrupt discontinuities in his work. At the same time, for the non-specialist, the monograph may serve as a highly accessible, even if somewhat partial, introduction to basic ideas of Parsons' highly complex theory of action, a body of theory often regarded as especially difficult to access. It provides an excellent source for beginning the study of the works of one of the few most creative and influential theorists of twentieth-century sociology.

Actor, Situation and Normative Pattern

An Essay in the Theory of Social Action *

Talcott Parsons

I. The Frame of Reference

In a recent book *The Structure of Social Action* (New York: McGraw-Hill, 1937), the present writer put forward the thesis that an important group of thinkers in the field of "social theory" had, without any important mutual influence on one another, converged in their work on a single unified theoretical system for the statement and analysis of certain of the most important of the facts of human social life. This system was called the "theory of action." Convergence was not equally on all logically important aspects of a system of empirical scientific theory, but on the basic frame of reference and on the account of the main elements of the structure of the empirical systems which are to be described and analyzed.

The object of this book was, by a careful and meticulous analysis of the works of four men, to disentangle the outline of the system from the varying approaches, differences in form of statement and in the empirical interests of the different writers, to show its bearings in relation to their empirical problems, and to demonstrate fully the fact of convergence. The accomplishment of these tasks required an extensive and difficult treatment in the course of which it is easy to lose sight of the main logical structure as a whole. Hence there is something to be said

* Courtesy of the Harvard University Archives, Talcott Parsons Papers.

for an attempt to outline this structure directly without reference to the critical context which was necessarily so prominent in the book.

Furthermore, when a study is made so intensively with reference to a particular critical context, a high degree of preoccupation with certain approaches and modes of statement which are particularly crucial in the critical understanding of the writers concerned is inevitable. Time and further thought from various points of view may well make possible a certain amount of simplification, and a somewhat altered approach and form of statement which makes the whole thing more generalized and, perhaps, more comprehensible to a reader who has not been through the critical material in detail. The object of the present essay is to attempt a systematic and generalized statement of the theoretical system without critical references. Like the critical statement in the earlier book, it will be confined to a brief statement of the frame of reference and an outline of the structure of systems. No systematic attention will be paid to the definition of analytic elements or variables. [1] Furthermore attention will be confined to statement. Systematic justification on either methodological or empirical grounds is impossible within the limits of such a brief treatment.

Biological theory, in the course of its long history, has developed a schema of thought which can, in certain aspects of its logical structure, serve as a point of departure for the present discussion. For it, all relevant phenomena are treated as pertaining to an organism or to its environment or both. The organism is a basic unit of reference even though it is treated, not as a simple thing, but as a highly complex system. Similarly, we may speak of the theory of action as always concerned with one or more such basic units of reference, human individuals, who, in this context, will be called "actors." [2] The actor is a complex system, but

---

1 The categories which define the structural elements of a system may or may not also define variables. Many of the categories of structure defined herein will doubtless be useful as variables in various different contexts. But the *systematic* intention of the present essay is not the definition of variables, but working out the structure of empirical systems.

2 "Context" here means within the frame of reference of action. The actor is a unit

can nevertheless, like the organism, be treated as an independent unit by contrast with its "situation."

The basic schema of organism and environment is employed in biology on at least two different levels. On the one hand, the unit of reference is what, in the empirical system in question, is a concrete unit, the concrete organism. On the other hand, biological theory proceeds for many of its most important purposes to another, an "analytical" level. Here, in the usual terminology, the unit of reference is not the organism, but its "hereditary constitution." The schema is not that of *organism* and environment, but of *heredity* and environment. The distinction is necessitated by the fact that, on the analytical level, the concrete organism is in important respects the product of "environmental" influences. Similarly, we may speak of actor and situation on two levels. On the one hand, it is a question of the concrete human individual, so far as he is relevant to the action frame of reference, acting in a concrete situation. On the other hand, analysis shows that the concrete "personality" is in large measure the product of past situational factors, so that on a generalized analytical level, methodologically comparable to that of the theory of heredity, the line must be drawn differently. The "actor" is no longer a concrete unit of an empirical system, even as described within the frame of reference of action, but an analytical abstraction.

In the case of both conceptual schemes, on both levels, it is possible to speak of a certain basic mode of relation between the two main conceptual components. In biology it is a matter of the "adaptation" of the organism to the environment. In order not to confuse the two frames of reference here the term "orientation" of the actor to his situation will be used. Consideration of what this means best starts on the concrete level of application of the conceptual scheme in question.

The essence of it would seem to be that the unit in question, the organism, for instance, is conceived as a "going concern." It is charac-

---

for purposes of description and analysis of systems of action. The actor is not a physical thing nor an organism since these are units in other frames of reference. See *The Structure of Social Action* (New York: McGraw-Hill, 1937), Chapters I and XIX.

terized by certain patterns of structure and function which, as a matter of sheer empirical observation, it tends to go through or maintain. The specific content of these patterns is not definable in general terms, but will vary according to the particular empirical problem. On the "physiological" level of biological analysis it is certain patterns of the organism at a given stage of the life cycle. On another level, it may be broadened to include the life cycle, or a significant sector of it. On still another, involving several generations, it may be a matter of the "species type." Finally, in evolutionary theory, changes in the species type are taken into account. But on all these levels the same common schema is involved, the conception of a relatively independent "form-pattern" of the organism which is maintained or approximated in its relations to the environment.

Given the fact that the organism is a "going concern," and that it has certain observable properties, and a given form-pattern, the continuance of its "life" or its "functioning" is dependent on a system of mutual interrelationships with the environment. One way of looking at this system is to consider the environment as offering a set of "conditions" to which the organism is "adapted." Thus the chemical processes of organic life being what they are, a continual chemical interchange with the environment is essential to the continuance of life. When it is possible to treat an aspect of this system of interrelation with the environment as a relatively independent system, this sub-system becomes one of the adaptive "functions" of the organism. Thus for the higher organisms, on a physiological level, nutrition, respiration and elimination are generally treated as distinct functions. A function may here be tentatively defined as a mode in which an organism meets essential conditions, in a given environment, of maintaining or carrying out, an observable characteristic form-pattern. From the point of view of the organism as a whole, all functions are adaptive. But the organism is a complex system. Insofar as it has a determinate structure some parts of it will constitute a relatively fixed "environment" to which the functioning of other parts must be "adapted." * So it is possible to speak of internal functions of the organism, as modes of adaptation of a restricted part of the organism to the conditions imposed by the determinate structure of the rest.

The essentials of this schema, in terms of logical structure, not of specific content, are applicable to action. An actor may be conceived as a "going concern" characterized by certain observable patterns [3] that are not directly reducible to terms of the situation in which he acts. In terms of the individual actor we generally, in common parlance, treat these patterns as his "character traits." As in the case of the organism, there is a complex system of interrelations between this unit, the actor, and his situation. Given what his dominant patterns are, in their maintenance or realization certain conditions are imposed upon him by the features of the situation. Every action- system of an individual will include functionally significant modes of orientation to the features of the situation, which are capable of relatively independent treatment as subsystems. No more than in the biological case will the specific functionally significant modes of action be uniform in all cases or all "species," but the functional analysis is one way of guiding the search for uniformities in action.

For present purposes, there seem to be two differences between the two fields which are of prime methodological importance. In the first place the theory of action is stated in terms of a frame of reference which involves "subjective categories," that is, which describes and analyzes things "from the point of view of the actor." That there is such a thing as the "state of mind" of the actor as a unit of reference of these subjective categories is a necessary methodological postulate, though it

---

* Here Parsons penned in a marginal note on his personal copy: Integrative question – V.L.

3 These "patterns" must, as will appear in the course of the discussion, be treated on two levels in the theory of action. On the one hand, there are certain directly empirically observable tendencies for the actor to maintain a pattern independent of the situation. On the other hand, analytically as seen in terms of the theory of action, this involves an "orientation" to "normative" patterns. The normative and the empirical patterns are related but by no means identical, since the latter are, analytically considered, resultants of normative and non-normative elements.

is not necessary to make any further ontological assumptions as to the ultimate nature of this entity. There is no analogy in biological theory to the role of the subjective in the theory of action.[4] It is because of this that it has seemed best to use different terms, actor instead of organism, situation instead of environment. This ensures clear recognition of the fact that *the two are analytically distinct conceptual schemes with no presumption of reducibility of either to the other* in spite of the far-reaching logical similarities. Even though there is an obvious empirical solidarity between the units of action and of biological systems, in that an actor is always empirically also an organism, it does not follow that the two "aspects" are identical, or that either is more "fundamental" than the other.

Closely associated with the subjective reference of the theory of action is another point. An essential element in both conceptual schemes has been called a set of form-patterns of the concrete units of systems. For the case of action these form patterns acquire an additional specification. Some of them, at least, have, for purposes of the action *analysis*, "normative" significance *to the actor*.[5] For one essential component of the processes of action as analyzed in terms of this scheme is what is variously described as "choice," "decision," etc. If this be true, it

---

4 There is, however, an element of analogy in the fact that, as it is sometimes put, the organism involves "teleological" elements of pattern independent of the environment. Biological theory does not, however, formulate these elements in "subjective" terms.

5 Such phrases as "subjective significance to the actor" should not be taken to imply that any given concrete actor is clearly "conscious" of the "meaning" imputed to him. The essential question is not whether what is, either to common sense or to some metaphysical system, an ontological entity like the "conscious mind" of the actor, to which a statement of facts refers, actually "exists." The concept of "state of mind" is rather "operational." It refers to the kind of subject matter in application to which a certain kind of observational procedures in terms of a certain frame of reference can be shown to "work", i.e., to yield verifiable knowledge. The area of which this is true is, experience shows, considerably broader than that of "consciousness" in common sense terms. This is perhaps best shown by the role of the "unconscious" in psychopathology, which is definitely formulated in "subjective" terms. But there are numerous other examples.

would seem to follow that there are two sets of considerations relevant to choices, the "conditional" and the "normative." The attempt to treat all considerations as conditional eliminates the conception of choice itself, and reduces the phenomena in question to terms of some other conceptual scheme than that of action.[6]

The other essential difference from the biological scheme is the role in action of the "social" aspect. While there are social organisms and biology may be said to have displayed considerable interest in the relations of organisms to one another, this interest is, at the same time, peripheral to biology. There is nothing in the conceptual scheme of action as such to prevent consideration of individual actors in relation to a non-social situation. But empirically the case where other actors are essential in the situation of a given one, is surely much more prominent than that where other organisms are treated as an essential part of the environment of the one which is the center of attention. One may say that virtually[7] the whole science of physiology may be formulated without any specific reference to the *relations* between organisms of the same species.

At any rate the principal interest of the present essay is in *social* systems of action which comprise a plurality of actors. For a conceptual scheme the main unit of reference of which is the state of mind of the individual actor this introduces considerable analytical complications. Certain of them will be discussed at appropriate points. For the present it will suffice to call attention to the fact that the implications of this fact are very much involved in the problem of transition from the concrete to the analytical levels of application of the scheme. For, from the point of view of any one concrete actor, all the other actors as concrete units are part of his situation of action. But in the analysis of a social system of action as a whole, this cannot be generalized. The logic of generalization in this context requires the transfer of certain elements from the situational to the pattern or normative category. In detail the possibili-

6 See *The Structure of Social Action, op. cit.*, Chapters. II and XII.

7 The main exception is, of course, the physiology of reproduction.

ties of error from failing to take proper account of this are numerous and subtle.

The starting point of the present statement, then, will be an attempt to isolate a few of the primary functional modes of relation of the actor to his situation and to normative patterns, and through this analysis to formulate the structurally most significant elements both of the situation of action and of the normative patterns of action. In doing this, it will be necessary successively to consider two different levels of analysis, that of the conceptually isolated individual actor, and that of the relations of such actors in social systems of action.

The frame of reference which has just been outlined requires the treatment of actor and situation in mutual interrelation. The actor in this context is defined as an entity oriented to normative patterns and to a situation at the same time. Put somewhat differently, the actor, like the organism, shows a certain independence of his environment or situation. He does not merely "react" to its stimuli, but he "takes advantage" of the situation to further his goals and normative tendencies. The relation to the situation is a selective one, not merely a dependent one. The actor is "teleologically" directed, but in terms capable of subjective formulation. It is this subjectivity of the frame of reference of action which makes necessary the distinction, with no biological analogue, between the subjective unit of reference, the "self," and the relevant normative patterns. Both normative patterns and situation are in some sense, though a different one in each of the two cases, "external" to the unit of reference.

II. The Three Basic Modes of Orientation: Cognitive, Teleological, Affectual

The present concern is with the primary functionally significant modes of relation between an actor, the relevant normative patterns, and his situation. For present purposes, it seems convenient to distinguish three such basic modes of orientation. These will involve the relation to normative patterns in somewhat different ways. Finally, on the basis of this analysis, it will be possible to distinguish aspects of the situation which are functionally significant to action and in terms of the interrelations of the functional modes of orientation, and the different aspects of the situation, both taken in relation to normative patterns, it will be possible to develop the main outline of the structure of social systems of action.

The first mode of relation of actor to situation, which is quite clearly basic, is the cognitive. Many elements essential to the understanding of action are most conveniently thought of as the answers to *questions* on the part of, or from the point of view of, the actor. These answers in the nature of the case are formulated as propositions. Propositions consist of concatenations of linguistic symbols with reference to some "reality." In a large class of cases undoubtedly the main symbolic reference is to some object in or aspect of the situation of action. But it does not follow that this is exclusively the case. The reference may be to the cognitive clarification of the goals, ends, purposes, or wishes of the actor himself or of normative patterns. [8]

---

[8] A word of explanation of the use of the term "cognitive" is here called for. It is an aspect of the "operational" use of a subjective category. We may speak of cognitive orientation whenever it is possible to contribute to the understanding of a course of action by saying of the actor, "He knew that ... " or "He thought that ... " In some cases there is evidence of clear self-conscious awareness; in others not. In particular there is a large class of "skills" in which adaptations *are* made to a changing situation without directing attention explicitly to it. Often the actor can attain retrospective awareness, but by no means always. Cognitive orientation will be treated

In distinguishing the cognitive from other aspects of the subjective aspect of action there is one peculiar difficulty, about which a word needs to be said. The theory of action, like all other theories of empirical science, is a body of knowledge. Hence, it is part of the cognitive orientation of some of the members of the society in which it is held. Furthermore, since the theory of action is couched in terms of subjective categories, it is knowledge of both the cognitive and the non-cognitive elements in the states of mind of actors. But the social scientist, in this respect, is himself an actor. What he is doing self-consciously on a level of more or less high methodological sophistication is only a relatively extreme case of what every actor does – to reflect in cognitive terms about his action as a whole. Hence every element or aspect of action *can* be stated in terms of the cognitive element from the point of view of the actor; it is methodologically possible to treat the whole of action in terms of cognitive orientation. [9] In that case the important analytical distinctions become matters of differences in content and methodological type of cognition.

If, then, a distinction between cognitive and non-cognitive aspects of action is to be used, it must be in terms of a highly "functional" point of view. The distinction is only tenable on a *given* analytical level and for

---

as an element in such action so long as its analytical use "works," ignoring the question of whether, in some other sense, the actor "knew" or "thought" what is imputed to him. The test of whether it works is whether, *in terms of the action scheme*, his holding a different belief or none at all would make a difference empirically.
It has been pointed out that one essential feature of cognitive orientation is the capability of linguistic formulation from the actor's point of view. It is quite possible, even certain, that elements of orientation by "experience," such as, "conditioned reflexes" that occur on a pre-linguistic level in animals and very young children, are concretely involved. In the absence of evidence to the contrary, it may, however, be assumed that these elements are integrated with the linguistic level and the latter may safely be used as a basis for the formulation of at least one essential variable.
On certain aspects of cognitive orientation, see the author's paper, "The Role of Ideas in Social Action," *American Sociological Review*, 3 (5): 652-664 (October, 1938).

9 This is probably one important source of the common "rationalistic" bias in social theory.

given analytical purposes. It is, in an even more drastic sense than applies to all scientific distinctions, not of direct ontological significance.

Recognizing the relativity of the distinction between cognitive and non-cognitive, for purposes of the theory of action, it seems important to distinguish two non-cognitive aspects or modes of orientation of the actor. One is that of teleological directionality. Directly it is not a mode of orientation to the situation at all, but to normative patterns. The above statement applies to that aspect of teleological directionality which is peculiar to the analytical interests of the theory of action. Another aspect of the concrete problem will have to be taken up presently.

Norms or normative patterns are, from the subjective point of view, in a sense "external realities" to the actor. Perhaps the best proof of this statement is the fact that they can be, and continually are, treated as objects of cognition by the actor. But in any given analytical context it is necessary to distinguish them from situational objects. From the cognitive point of view situational elements can always be described in terms of existential propositions, even though, in reference to future situations, they refer to phenomena not existent at the time the proposition is enunciated. A normative pattern, on the other hand, does not, from the point of view of the actor, "exist" in the same sense. The propositions involved may, to be sure, describe a "state of affairs." But so far as their significance is normative it is not asserted (simply or at all) that this exists or, with a certain degree of probability, will exist, but that it *ought* (or ought not) to exist. The mood is imperative, not indicative. Whether it actually does or will come to exist is indifferent in principle to its normative status. What "exists" is the normative pattern, an "ideal" entity, not the state of affairs to which it refers.[10]

But though the immediate object of normative orientation is a normative pattern, indirectly it strongly affects the relation of the actor to the situation. For it is basic to the frame of reference of action that in comprehensive systems normative pattern and situation never com-

---

[10] See *The Structure of Social Action*, *op. cit.*, especially Chapter II, Note A and Chapter IX.

pletely and directly correspond. There is always a certain discrepancy and a corresponding tension.[11] Seen in its context as a guide to future action a normative pattern defines a state of affairs which in important respects would not come into existence at the requisite point of time if the empirically knowable trends of the situation were simply projected far enough into the future. To "realize" a normative pattern, it is essential that the actor should "intervene" in the situation, or should maintain a course of intervention already under way.[12] In the context of normative orientation, the actor is related to the situation as an active agent. The situation is to him a set of means and conditions[13] of attainment of his ends, or of obstacles to their attainment. He does not merely float along on the current of situational events, but changes, modifies, inhibits, and selects in relation to situational processes.

---

11 The tension is analytically independent of the discrepancy. Correspondence may be maintained by a high level of effort.

12 "Action" in the present sense means the results of any decision so far as they are significant to the subsequent course of events. A decision *not* to do something projected or considered is just as much "action" or "intervention" as is a decision to take positive measures.
A closely related point: action is the outcome of "decisions." A decision is always a *choice* between two or more alternative courses. The actor predicts his relation to the situation (i.e., the state of the "actor-situation system" for a given future time on the hypothesis of each of several projected possible courses. Each will involve different modes of "intervention" and will lead to different situations differently "desirable" in terms of the relevant normative patterns and interests, directly his "goals." The "choice" is an outcome of the balance between "predictions" and some kind of "maximization of utility" (in Pareto's broad sense – see *The Structure of Social Action, op. cit.*, Chapter VI). The case of "choice" of means to a *given* end is a special case. The end or goal is isolated from others either in that it is absolutized or that it is assumed the action will have a negligible effect on other ones – an assumption which varies widely in empirical justification. The choice of means is then limited to its relevance to the degree of attainment of this particular end and its immediate "costs." The concepts of "efficiency" and "cost" are discussed below, pp. 64 ff. See Louis Wirth, *American Sociological Review*, 4 (3): 399-404 (June 1939). [The reference is to Wirth's review of Talcott Parsons' *The Structure of Social Action* (*op. cit.*) – V.L.].

13 Strictly only at the pole of rationality. See below pp. 71ff.

The aspect of teleological directedness that is of peculiar analytical importance to the theory of action would seem to be that which has just been summed up as normative orientation, the acceptance or rejection of normative patterns. But this does not exhaust the teleological directedness of concrete action as a whole. The relation of this element to another is one of the most important sources of analytical difficulty in the whole field and must now be taken up.

For the analytical purposes of the theory of action, the actor is not a biological organism because he is a unit in a frame of reference different from that of biological theory. But experience shows that he is a unit in a peculiarly close and intimate relationship to one biological organism, the actor's own "body." This is not the place to enter into the involved problem of "body-mind" relationships. [14] Two facts are important here: the fact that concretely the two are "aspects" of a single concrete entity, the human "individual," and that, in the terms in use here, they are aspects of which neither is in any simple sense "reducible" to terms of the other.

From the point of view of the action schema, the actor's own body is part of the *situation* of that actor, which he treats in essentially the same terms as the "external" situation. But, at the same time, there are certain differences. Seen in its relations to the physical world, to its "environment," the human organism, like other organisms, is a teleologically directed entity. It is a system, which is, within certain limits, [15] independent of environmental conditions. It has, then, certain teleological tendencies which are not analytically derivable from the normative patterns to which the actor is oriented.

But the concrete unit of action systems is not the analytically abstracted "actor;" it is the human "individual." Insofar as this concrete unit is teleologically directed, its concrete teleological tendencies are analytically composite; they are partly, from the point of view of the

[14] Most of the discussion of this problem is on a metaphysical level which is irrelevant here.

[15] Cf. W. B. Cannon, *The Wisdom of the Body* (New York: Norton, 1939).

theory of action, modes of normative orientation, partly the outcome of biologically given "drives." The latter may have subjective manifestations, like all classes of elements determining action, but for analytical purposes they must be classed as situational elements.

It is necessary to make one or two further remarks about the mode of relation between the biological drive element of teleological directedness and the normative element. A general tendency to empiricism, which has been prevalent in the social sciences, has often led to making this distinction the basis of a classification of the concrete "wants" or ends of man; there are, on the one hand, his instinctive or biological needs, like hunger, sex, self-preservation, and the like, on the other hand, his "higher" wants like religion, aesthetic satisfactions, the dictates of conscience, and the like. This, as an immense amount of evidence shows, clearly will not do. There is not a single class of concrete wants or ends, no matter how "high" and apparently removed from the biological level, in which there is not a presumption that biological elements play an important part. Psychoanalysis may be said to have demonstrated this beyond any reasonable doubt. But, at the same time, a point about which psychoanalytic theorists have not been so clear, even in the most definitely "biological" of human wants, like that for food and sexual satisfaction, normative elements can be demonstrated to play a decisive role in determining the specific forms, not only of their satisfaction, but of the wants themselves.

The correct way to conceive the relation would seem to be not that there are separate biological and "cultural" wants, but that there are two analytically distinct classes of elements in all concrete wants. Above all the biological element does not define concrete wants at all, but only certain underlying "vectors" of direction of teleological tendencies. In detail, the distinction is always an empirical question to be investigated in terms of the specific facts.

Another common conception is that, in general terms, the biological element is "antisocial" and that the sole function of normative patterns is to suppress or control our biological tendencies. There is a grain of truth in this view, but as a generalized statement of the relation, it is untenable. The grain of truth lies in the fact that in this, as in other aspects, normative patterns and situational elements are never perfectly "congruent" and there is, hence, always an element of tension between the two. But this does not mean that there is no important element of relative congruence in this area, any more than that there is no such thing as an aspect of the "fitness of the environment" in relation both to the organism and the actor. Above all, it should never be assumed that when there are concrete wishes or elements of them which are in opposition to concrete normative patterns, these are necessarily manifestations of biological drives in a simple sense. [16] The subtle interdependence and combination of biological and normative elements exists at many different levels in the complex structure of personality, and it may be said with considerable confidence that in practically all cases of concrete wishes which come into conflict with social norms, analysis will reveal normative pattern elements of crucial importance in the wishes themselves. Even the Freudian "infantile" levels of sexuality to which neurotic individuals may regress are by no means necessarily the manifestations of purely biological tendencies.

Still a third common conception is that the directive "energy" of teleologically directed action always has biological sources, and that the function of normative structures is to provide a "form" within which this organic energy works. There seems to be no adequate evidence for this view. Unquestionably the problem of analysis of the "energy" of action is complex, but there is no obvious reason for deriving it exclusively from biological sources. Perhaps this tendency of thought derives in part from the conception that all "energy" is ultimately physico-chemical in nature and that the source of "motivation" in action must ultimately lie in the physical energy liberated by the processes of oxidation in organic metabolism. But if the biological and the action conceptual schemes

16 A prominent example of the tendency to make this assumption is the derivation of aggressions from the "death instinct." For a critique of this concept, see Karen Horney, *New Ways in Psychoanalysis* (New York: Norton, 1939), Chapter VII.

are, in fact, analytically independent in any degree, there is no reason on general grounds why the "driving forces" of concrete action should be of a nature to be exclusively accessible to conceptual formulation in biological terms and in no sense so subject in terms specific to the theory of action. A scientifically cautious student of the theory of action will avoid any gratuitously *a priori* theorems [17] of this character.

Whatever the sources of the "energy" or "force" of action processes, in teleological directedness, there would seem to be two primary aspects. On the one hand, there is a kind of "energy potential," a level of intensity in the realization of normative patterns, partly helped along by biological drives, partly in spite of, or in opposition to, them. On the other hand, there is the aspect by virtue of which the direction of teleological orientation is defined. In both aspects, teleological directionality may be treated as a resultant of variables, but different ones in the two cases.

In the history of thought a particularly prominent part in the analysis of teleological directionality has been played by the concepts of "end" and the "means-end relationship." Important as the means-end schema is, it does not seem to be sufficiently general to find a place in the most general schema of orientation of action. It is apparently essentially a polar type within the broader category of teleological directionality. Insofar as teleological tendencies become clearly and sharply formulated from a cognitive point of view and approach a maximum of self-consciousness on the part of the actor, they are best analyzed in means-end terms, with the directional elements formulated as ends. But short of this, there are many teleological aspects of action that should not be overlooked or squeezed into other categories, because they do not exactly fit the specific means-end schema. A suitable more general term is "goal."

As is the case with other aspects of the theory of action, the status of the means-end schema is different on different analytical levels. On the most concrete level, an "end" is analytically a composite; it formulates

[17] The Freudian "libido" theory seems to have a large *a priori* element of this character.

both normative and biological elements of teleological directionality in combination with each other and with a cognitive orientation to the relevant situational factors. It is only on a more generalized analytical level, which regards the biological element as situational, that a distinction between biological and normative aspects of teleological directionality becomes feasible or important. When this level is reached, the teleological content of ends becomes exclusively normative leaving in addition only a cognitive grasp of the relevant aspects of the situation.

It must not, however, be assumed that normative elements do not play an important part in the diffuser "non-logical" modes of teleological directionality. On the contrary, this mode of relation to action, through "sentiments" or "value-attitudes," is probably quantitatively much more important than in the mode of clearly formulated ends.

In contrast to normative patterns, which are in a sense "external" and objective in relation to the actor, "emotional" or "affective" attitudes are specifically subjective. This is a difficult and somewhat obscure subject, but certain fundamental things can be said. The first important point relates to the three-fold structure of affective attitudes which may be called, "positive," "negative," and neutral. By positive attitudes is meant such as we usually describe as liking, acceptance, love, respect, and the like, by negative such as dislike, rejection, hatred, or contempt. At both ends of this polarity, there are certainly important bases of variation; for instance, affection and respect, while both positive attitudes are by no means identical, nor are hatred and contempt, though both are negative. What is here meant by affective neutrality seems to be in one respect the midpoint of the positivenegative polarity; it is defined as an absence of either positive or negative affects. But it is doubtful whether this aspect of the matter is a sufficient basis for analysis. Perhaps the other elements consist in a mode of relation of the affective to other, cognitive or teleological, aspects of the structure of action. In any case a control of affective tendencies in either direction, hence approximation to neutrality, is often a positive requirement of action patterns. Thus, in scientific investigation affects of either type are felt to be a hindrance, as they are in certain types of technologically or economically rational action.

There are three polarities which are closely related to the basic polarity of affects, which require specific comment. Though the old-fashioned kind of hedonism is no longer seriously adhered to, the pleasure-pain, or pleasure- unpleasure dichotomy plays so persistent a role in discussion of affective orientation that it would quite clearly appear to be something of fundamental importance. A good deal of evidence points to the view that analytically pleasure is primarily significant as a subjective manifestation of biological organic states. Probably Freud's concept of it as the result of stimulation of erogenous zones is too narrow, but his basic orientation to the problem seems acceptable.

It may be objected to this view, that many states, and the gratification of many wishes, appear to be pleasurable which are not in any obvious sense biological wishes. This objection seems to be met in part by consideration of the fact that no concrete wish is ever simply biological or wholly unbiological. In addition there is a further consideration. The concrete organism is never wholly the product of what are, analytically considered, biological elements. An immense accumulation of evidence from medical sources has gone to show that "psychic" influences are of crucial importance in the determination even of organic pathological states, such as, gastric ulcers, various heart lesions, and the like. [18] If this is possible, even of conspicuous structural changes of the organism, there would seem to be no objection on general grounds to the interpretation of pleasure as the subjective manifestation of a state of the concrete organism, even though that, in turn, is influenced to a high degree by other than biological factors. This statement should not be taken to mean that there are no important qualitative distinctions of different kinds of pleasure, or its opposite. It may, however, be concluded, that one of the primary elements of affective orientation to the

[18] Cf. especially H. Flanders Dunbar, *Emotions and Bodily Changes* (New York: Columbia University Press, 1935).

situation generally is the relation of objects, activities and results to the pleasure-unpleasure balance of the organism.

The second component of affective orientation, which calls for special comment here, and which plays a crucial analytical role in the theory of action, is what may be called "moral respect" and its antithesis, moral indignation. In the first instance, this may be identified as an empirically specific element which has risen into prominence because, within the frame of reference of action, it has again and again been empirically necessary to take account of it. It may be said to have the same subjective specificity of status (*Evidenz* in German) that pleasure has; everyone has the experience of moral respect, and its antithesis, as is the case with pleasure and pain. But the question arises whether it is not possible to go somewhat further to establish some of its general relations to the structure of action.

As distinguished from pleasure and pain, the context of moral respect and its antithesis is specifically normative. It would, of course, be arbitrary to assume that it was the only significant affective correlate of normative patterns, but its peculiar relevance to them seems beyond doubt. Moral indignation has a place only in the context of violation of normative patterns to which the actor in question feels attached. Another sense in which moral respect has peculiar relation to normative patterns is shown by a certain "impersonality" which attaches to it. Moral feelings seem to attach in the first instance to matters of "principle" and to particular persons, objects, etc. only insofar as they embody relatively abstract and general principles. Typical objects of moral feelings are such things as "honesty," "loyalty," etc., and in justifying a moral judgment of a person we habitually refer to such principles – we are indignant at him because he has acted "dishonestly," for instance.

The part of the complex of action which is constituted on the one hand by the content of at least a vital sector of normative patterns, on the other by the affective attitudes of moral respect and indignation, is the heart of what will, in discussing the theory of action, be called the "value" complex. An exceedingly crucial place in the structure of both the individual personality and of social systems is occupied by this complex, or the "value-orientation" either of a particular actor or of a plurality of actors in common.

Value-orientation is not wholly subjective in character in the sense that it is closely interdependent with a certain class of situational elements, particularly as cognitively apprehended. In particular, it is very closely bound up with that aspect of the cognitive orientation to the situation which will be spoken of later as "religious ideas." This aspect cannot be discussed further until we come to the relation of these particular modes of orientation to particular aspects of the situation, and hence to the analysis of more specific "structuralizations" of the three basic orientation modes.

The third polarity in the affective field seems to lie on a different level and, though it may contain elements of the other two, is yet of peculiar significance. It is that most commonly known as the polarity of "love" and "hate." Unlike pleasure and pain, it is not a "subjective" thing with no reference beyond the actor and his body except to a cause or "stimulus." Unlike moral respect its focus is not on abstract normative principles, but on particular persons and things as such. There are doubtless many nuances at both poles and this is not the place to attempt to distinguish them. The specific terms used do not matter. But there would appear to be a general affective orientation of "attraction" to a person or thing, or perhaps also in certain respects "identification" with it (especially if a person), and on the other hand repulsion, antagonism, and the like. This mode of orientation is ordinarily integrated with the other two basic affective polarities. We doubtless tend on the whole to "love" or be attracted to persons or things with which we associate actual or prospective pleasurable experiences, and which exemplify moral principles of which we approve. Yet, the subtle analyses of the emotions in fiction are full of cases of relative dissociation of these three modes of affective orientation, any one from the other two, so it would not seem possible to avoid treating them as analytically independent, however closely interdependent empirically.

This list of three is, naturally, not necessarily exhaustive, but there does seem to be warrant for considering it rather fundamental. For example, there is considerable evidence for this in the later work of Freud. The "pleasure principle" as Freud treats it is clearly distinguishable analytically from the moral element which Freud localizes in the "superego."[19] The status of "love" in Freud is more difficult to interpret. Perhaps in his earlier work it tended to be identified with the pleasure principle. But in the later work the latter tends to become more and more definitely biological, associated directly with the stimulation of erogenous zones (surely too narrow a concept for present purposes), and to be distinguished from "object cathexis." In the latter connection there is a mode of identification with the love object which, though empirically greatly influenced by its role as a source of pleasure, surely is not a mere reflex of the pleasure principle.

Another example is the work of W. I. Thomas. Here, for some reason, the pleasure principle does not appear specifically, but seems to diffuse through all four of the wishes. Two of the latter, the wishes for new experience and for security, are clearly on a different analytical level from the modes of affective orientation now under discussion. The other two, the wishes for recognition and for response, fit the above analysis very well. Recognition is, it may be said, the reciprocal of moral respect. Recognition from others is the correlate of the moral respect the actor gives to others when they embody approved patterns, and is a measure of his own achievement in realizing values.[20] Response, on the other hand, is specifically different. Instead of being "impersonal" as recognition is, it can be enjoyed only from a particular individual, and has a clearly different affective tone. The difference from the above formulation lies in two facts. On the one hand, Thomas thinks of affects projected upon the actor who is the point of reference by others, not from him upon other objects. On the other hand, Thomas considers response only in re-

---

19 Along with the moral element in a generalized analytical sense this Freudian concept involves certain elements derived from his conception of child development which are of much more dubious status. Cf. Horney (*op. cit.*), Chapter XIII.

20 Cf. below pp. 104ff for an analysis of this relation.

lation to persons, whereas a very similar affective tone exists in relation to objects. Also, Thomas considers only one side of the polarity.

Before leaving affective orientation, it should be noted that, in all three of the respects noted, there may be very complex interrelations on the symbolic level between the objects of affective attitudes. Freudian psychoanalysis has immensely illuminated these connections, though it does not seem correct to accept the Freudian "one way" theory of symbolic relationships; on the contrary, they often seem to be reciprocal in many different ways. But the Freudian view that such relationships are often far below the threshold of consciousness is undoubtedly correct.

III. The Structure of the Situation as an Object of the Orientation of Action

A. The Situation as Object of Cognition

The above analysis is made entirely in terms of the actor as a point of reference. It deals with the primary features of the actor which are of significance in terms of his process of interaction with the situation. But this is only half of the basic analytical picture. It is now necessary to turn to the analysis of the situation. But just as, in analyzing the actor, attention was centered on those things of primary significance for his relations to the situation, here the analysis of the situation will be in terms of its structure precisely as a situation *of action*, not as a "physical" world or from any other point of view.[21]

In the first instance, then, the situation is an object or system of objects of cognition. In this connection, the history of the theory of action in Western Europe in the past few centuries has concentrated overwhelmingly on one particular mode of cognition, and a corresponding classification of situational objects. The central point of reference of Western thought has been empirical science, and it is as an object of scientific knowledge that, in the cognitive mode, we have been most concerned with the situation of action. In this connection the situation may be called an empirical system. It is such insofar as it serves as an object of empirical cognition, all the way from the simplest and most naive common sense to the most sophisticated forms of modern science.

There would seem, actually, to be no other equally clear positively defined category of objects of cognition,[22] so that it seems justified to

---

[21] The approach here taken is very similar to that of Dr. H. A. Murray in his concept of "press." See his *Explorations in Personality* (New York: Oxford University Press, 1938).

[22] There is one system of thought common in Western history which, in principle, reduces the possible modes of cognitive orientation to one alone – namely, em-

speak of the residual category of the "non-empirical" situation. This would include, so far as they are relevant to this context, the objects of Revelation, theological and metaphysical speculation, mystical experience, and the like. Certain distinctions within it will be made below in terms of functional relations to the other modes of the orientation of the actor than the cognitive. The use of these modes as bases of cognitive distinctions is justified by the fact that there is no concrete orientation without cognitive elements, and vice versa, no cognition without relation to the other modes of orientation.

It should be noted that the methodological position underlying this discussion is "non-positivistic."[23] It is the defining characteristic of positivism that it radically denies the possibility of significant cognitive propositions outside the realm of empirical science. Treatment of non-empirical cognition as a residual category should not be taken to mean that it is analytically unimportant or, what amounts to the same thing, that its content varies at random.

There are certain kinds of action where the cognitive mode of orientation is, though not isolated, dominant. Scientific investigation and philosophical speculation are the two principal cases. But more often another mode occupies the dominant place, and the cognitive stands in

---

pirical science. This, the "positivistic" system, has been exhaustively analyzed in *The Structure of Social Action*, *op. cit.*, especially Chapters. II, III, V, and IX. No position is taken here on the metaphysical status of this system but, in terms of the scientific frame of reference of action, it can quite justly be claimed to be inadequate in that it fails to make empirically important distinctions. There are, demonstrably important to action, "ideas" which are neither elements of *valid* empirical knowledge, nor are they "wrong" when judged by standards of empirical validity, they are "non-empirical," not subject to empirical verification. A positivistic theory of action must somehow alter the conceptual scheme so as adequately to take account of these *facts* without leaving a place for other than empirical cognition. The present author is unaware of any way in which this can be done.

[23] It should not be inferred that "ideas" about such subjects do not, *along with* cognitive grasp of non-empirical aspects of the situation, state or imply erroneous conceptions of empirical phenomena. This is very common indeed. The category of "ideas of the non-empirical situation" is an analytical category. Any concrete system of ideas may well contain other elements.

an instrumental position. Much the most familiar of these is the rational teleological context of the processes of seeking to attain specific empirical ends. It is inherent in the structure of the means-end schema that two types of cognitive problems should be involved in it, and hence two types of situational objects of cognition. On the one hand, action requires knowledge of the empirical situation; of its predicted future trends of development and of the probable effects of various alternative ways of altering or abstaining from altering this trend. These are questions of "ways and means." To our traditions of thought the empirical situation seems to be the only one relevant to ways and means of attaining ends. In many societies, however, knowledge of the ways of non-empirical entities and forces is thought highly important in just these connections, as in the form of "magical theories."

But this does not exhaust the cognitive problems involved in the pursuit of ends. There is, in addition, the problem of justification of the pursuit of the end in the first place. In part, within a system of means-end relationships, this can take place by reference to further and further ramifications of the system, but ultimately this resource fails and recourse must, logically, be had to non-empirical considerations, particularly to philosophical conceptions of the place of man in the universe and the meaning of his existence. So even a "purely rational" system of action cannot, from the cognitive point of view, be confined to knowledge of empirical objects alone. [24]

Seen in terms of the frame of reference of action this means that insofar as cognition is thought of as subsidiary to teleological directedness, to the pursuit of goals, the situation is not analytically undifferentiated, but falls into two categories. On the one hand, there are those aspects of the situation which are approached in terms of the question *how* a given goal is to be achieved; on the other hand, those relevant to the question *why* it should be pursued. In the mode of rationality, which

---

[24] Cf. Pareto's treatment of the second abstract society following his theory of Social Utility, *The Mind and Society; A Treatise on General Sociology* (New York: Dover, 1935), paragraph 2141 ff. Cf. also *The Structure of Social Action*, *op. cit.*, Chapter VI, pp. 220 ff.

plays such a dominant part in Western thought, there can be no doubt of the central position of empirical knowledge in the first connection, though it is doubtful how far its *exclusive* relevance can, in view of the prevalence of magic, be upheld. In the second connection, there is every evidence that, even insofar as action tends to be "rational," the cognitive type approached is not that of empirical knowledge, certainly by no means alone, but rather that a crucial role is played by non-empirical, metaphysical ideas. At least one proposition is beyond any serious dispute: when systems of action in the teleological mode are described and analyzed in terms of the action schema, including the linguistic expressions of the cognitive orientation of the actors, there is no concrete system of action known where the relevant "ideas" can be treated adequately as consisting of either elements of valid empirical knowledge alone or of "ignorance and error" which has been superseded by the advance of empirical knowledge.[25] There is always an essential component left over which is decisive in this connection, but which must, when measured by the criteria of scientific validity, be judged to be *non*-scientific rather than *un*scientific. Pareto's work (among others) may be said to have demonstrated this beyond reasonable doubt. The demonstration runs all through his analysis of the ideas associated with action, but culminates in his theorem, in the theory of social utility, that even in a "rational" social system of action "essential data" are lacking that would be necessary for the conception of a "society based entirely upon reason."

Not only does cognition play an important role in contexts where the teleological mode of orientation is dominant, but also when it is subsidiary to the affective mode. Insofar as the affective mode is analytically isolated, the role of the actor would seem to be "passive" rather than "active." He does not "do" things, but things "happen to" him. But here also the basic dichotomy of questions, between the how and the why, reappears. The question of how things happen is, at least in one of its major aspects, referable to empirical knowledge, though it is perhaps

[25] Cf. the author's essay, "The Role of Ideas in Social Action," *op. cit.*

also referable to non-empirical contexts so far as magical theories prevail. But the question of why raises different problems. In the present connection, it is the question of "meaning" which is significant: what does it mean in an emotionally significant and satisfying sense, that such things happen? Analysis of actual social systems seems to show beyond reasonable doubt that the answers to such questions lead regularly over into non-empirical considerations.

There is a sense in which affective orientation is peculiarly bound up with the "self-interest" of the actor. In the case of the pleasure-unpleasure balance this seems to be obvious because these affects are specifically private and subjective. In the case of moral respect the decisive fact would seem to be that a moral principle is only of (positive or negative) affective significance to a person insofar as, in the Freudian term, it has been "introjected," as it is built into the structure of the individual personality, so that its violation has direct subjective consequences to the emotional balance and state of the individual, if he himself is the violator in the form of feelings of guilt or shame, if another, in the form of moral indignation. [26] Finally, in the case of love and hate, the actor tends to become in a sense "identified" with the particular object. In the positive mode, his affective state is bound up with its welfare or continued existence, with availability to him for enjoyment and, if human, or even animate, with its responsiveness to him. There are doubtless a number of different nuances in these "identifications," but common to them all is the dependence of the actor's affective state, his "happiness," on both the state of the loved object, and his relation to it, including its responsiveness to him.

Affective orientation to a situation is never divorced from cognitive orientation, knowledge, and cognitive grasp of those aspects of the situation which are affectively meaningful to the actor. So close is the association that a stable affective orientation would seem to presuppose some order of cognitive orientation to this range of problems, some kind

[26] In both cases these affects may work out on the unconscious level.

of answer to the problems of meaning which are inevitably implicit in the actor's relation to his situation.

But precisely because the roots of affective orientation lie so deep in the subtler foundations of personality, it is common in stable social situations for a high degree of traditionalization of the cognitive patterns to be found, so that, over a large area, the individual actor is scarcely conscious that there are problems of meaning, as he takes the traditional solutions of them completely for granted. [27] But a very high degree of stability in these respects is unusual. There are many inherent features of human action and its situation which subject the actor to unavoidable frustrations and to unexpected good fortune of affective significance. Certain of these are unusual from the point of view of the individual, but not of the society. This is true of the "crises of life" of which the most dramatic and upsetting is death. These crises are in all societies more or less the focus of specific mechanisms, [28] a main function of which can be interpreted to be the affective adjustment of individuals to an emotionally upsetting situation. Most of the mechanisms are ritual procedures, and *one* essential component in all of them is some kind of cognitive pattern oriented to the problem of the meaning of the occurrence or the situation in question.

But, at the same time, things are continually occurring which involve emotional strains and which are not adequately taken care of by such traditionally established mechanisms. In certain kinds of situations, these strains become acute in somewhat the same directions for large numbers of people. Cognitively, this may be the setting for new statements of, and new answers to, various aspects of the problem of meaning.

There is reason to believe that frustration of expected positive affectual interests is more important in this connection, though not of exclusive importance, than the attainment of unexpected or, according to

---

[27] Cf. Adolf Harnack, *Mission and Expansion of Christianity in the First Three Centuries* (New York: Putnam, 1908) on the way in which these things are taken for granted in an "established religion."

[28] The "Rites de Passage," made a classical term by Arnold van Gennep, *Rites de Passage* (Paris: Nourry, 1909).

prevailing moral standards, undeserved benefits. In a given social situation which is at all stable, there would seem to be established a kind of emotional equilibrium. This includes a structure of expectations of what will "happen to" the actor in various respects. It also includes expectations as to the success of goal-directed activities, of the relations between effort, skill, and outcome of actions, and of the recognition and response of others. These "legitimate" expectations are always to some degree rationalized in terms of the established cognitive orientation of the society to the problem of meaning.

But to varying degrees a given orientation will fail to give satisfactory understanding of the meaning of the grosser frustrations which develop, as also to varying degrees the problems themselves will be clearly grasped. In terms of the threefold structure of modes of affective orientation, there are three main aspects of the problem of the meaning of frustrations. Insofar as it is frustrations of expectations of pleasure, it is the "problem of suffering;" where it is a matter of moral conduct, and vice versa the avoidance of immorality is involved, it is the "problem of evil;" and finally frustrations of love form a third basic set of problems. Here it may take the form of legitimate expectations of response.

In all these connections, both the problems of how and of why are involved. The problem of how serves as the setting for an explanation of the source of frustration, and hence provides an object for focus of the negative affects which can be projected outward on the situation, moral indignation and hatred. But back of this lies the other mode of orientation, to the question of why. In its relation to personal agents, it is not the question of *who* did something, but of *why* in the sense of what were his motives, what did he *mean* by it.

In close relation to the problem of meaning, another basically important aspect of the cognitive relation to the situation enters in. Particularly insofar as the analytical starting point for the study of cognitive orientation is, as has been the case with so much of Western thought, the methodology of empirical science, the significance of objects known is thought of as lying in their "nature," in what they are and do. It is true that the language in terms of which this knowledge is expressed and communicated is a system of symbols, but they are symbols with a direct reference to "real" phenomena, to objects and relations. Relations between situational objects, or facts, are, on this level, casual relations, relations of intrinsic interconnectedness. But it is also possible to interpret objects and events themselves, not merely their linguistic symbols, as having symbolic significance, as being less important for their own sakes than for what they "mean."

No more than in the other cases dealt with is it safe to assume that for the purposes of the theory of action the category of "symbolic relationship" can be treated as homogeneous. One range of variation appears to be particularly significant. At one pole is the type which appears to be most important in scientific symbolization where the symbol is a purely arbitrary, conventionally accepted "sign," most conspicuous in mathematics and symbolic logic. On the semantic level, as opposed to the phonetic, this element is very conspicuous in ordinary as opposed to scientific language. At the opposite pole is the case where there is some order of "meaningful appropriateness" as opposed to complete arbitrariness, in the relation of symbol and referent, hence in the choice of symbol. One very important case of such symbolism is the expressional symbolism of the arts. But even this can be treated on more than one level so that further distinctions are necessary. One level is that of what may be called "unity of style." It is quite clear that a gothic pointed arch would be badly out of place between any two columns of the Parthenon, for instance, or a few bars of "swing" in the middle of "Nearer My God To Thee." But unity of style, in the arts or elsewhere, may or may not be referred to some kind of a motivational unity, or other deeper unity. The unity of a rational teleological system is not a case in point so long as the direct intrinsic means-end relationships can be traced. There is much evidence, notably in the phenomena of ritual, that teleological orientations make liberal use of symbolically significant acts and "properties." But perhaps the most important type of symbolic relation on the motivationally appropriate level is that in which acts have significance as symbolic expressions of affective attitudes. Of course, it should be understood that, along with the element of meaningful appropriateness, which is involved in such cases, there may also be one which is intrinsically arbitrary but has gained symbolic significance through "association" particularly in connection with the circumstances of the life-history of individuals. [29]

A type of symbolic relationship on the meaningfully appropriate level, which is in many respects structurally similar to the meaningful unity of human motivation, but analytically distinguishable from it, is that which is involved in conceptions of the meaningful basis of order in the universe, particularly in relation to the "supernatural." In many cases this tends to be assimilated to the conception of human motivation, but in others it is thought of as an impersonal though nonetheless meaningful principle of order. Also, in many cases, particularly where the supernatural entity is thought of as "personal" there is a tendency to conceive his "actions" on the model of the intrinsic means-end relationship. But even in these cases, we are dealing with limiting types and it is always well to keep the conception of a different principle, some kind of "symbolic expression," in mind as an analytical tool.

It should be noted again that the problem of meaning is a field in which cognitive elements not only never stand alone, but very often seem to be overshadowed by others. The primary basis of interest is often affective rather than cognitive. Often, when affects are strong, they seriously interfere with the efficiency of the cognitive process, and actors appear to be emotionally satisfied with solutions, on both levels, which, to a disinterested and competent analysis, are palpably absurd, are obviously "rationalizations," and the like. Moreover, this is precisely the field in which neurotic mechanisms are most prominent and one universal component of such mechanisms is the distortion of the cognitive picture of the situation, for instance, in the paranoid mechanism of imputing greatly exaggerated hostility and ill will to individuals in the

[29] These associations may, as psychoanalysis in particular has shown, be buried in the deeper layers of the "unconscious" and the individual may thus be unaware of them. This is probably not, as Freud would imply, confined to cases of the repression of one side of a conflict.

situation. But this does not destroy the analytic importance and independence of the cognitive aspect of orientation. Cognitive work on the problems of meaning can be shown to be a factor of major importance in historical change, in certain contexts and particularly over long periods of time.[30] The problem of the relation of basic cognitive orientation to the problem of meaning to the rationalizations of neurotic mechanisms is complex and cannot be fully discussed here. The one essential point is that cognitive orientation is functionally basic to "normal" systems of action, and cannot be treated as *only* a neurotic mechanism, and hence important only as a "distortion" of the actual situation. In Freud, the "reality principle" has an essential place as a counterfoil to the concept of rationalization.[31]

After reviewing these many distinctions from the cognitive point of view a tentative attempt may be made to systematize the material somewhat further. In "purely cognitive" terms, or more accurately those in which the cognitive interest is primary rather than instrumental, there appear to be two primary distinctions. On the one hand, there is what Pareto calls the "domain of observation and experience," on the other hand, what has above been called the realm of the "non-empirical." Admittedly the latter is a residual category but it does not seem necessary to attempt to analyze it further for present purposes. Secondly, there is the distinction according to directions of human interest in cognitive problems between the question "how" and the question "why," between the

[30] Moreover, neurotic distortions can only be understood by reference to a standard of "normal" orientation. On this influence, see Max Weber, *Gesammelte Aufsätze zur Religionssoziologie* (Tübingen: J.C.B. Mohr, 1922), which is by far the most extensive empirical analysis of the problem.

[31] As Professor A. D. Nock has stated (in lectures), no religion has ever pretended to be able to "beat death." Insofar as religion consists in a set of cognitive ideas about the meaning of such major frustrations as death, it is not a mere "escape mechanism" or rationalization in the psychopathological sense. [Arthur Darby Nock, 1902-1963, was Professor of Classics at Harvard University and the author of major works on early Christianity and on Hellenistic civilization. Nock lectured in Sociology 23, Parsons' course on Comparative Institutional Analysis in the 1930s. V.L.]

understanding of the "nature" of objects, events, experiences, and their "meaning."

The dominant analytical starting point for the analysis of cognitive orientation in the history of Western thought has been the methodology of empirical science. For present purposes, science or "empirical knowledge" may be said to be that aspect of cognitive orientation which arises in response to questions of how, with respect to the empirical world, or the domain of observation and experience. The other three possibilities of cognitive orientation would then, together, be relegated to another residual category, "philosophy," so far, that is, as the cognitive interest is dominant.

Now it is a conspicuous fact in the Western world that what is here called science does not consist in an entirely discrete agglomeration of miscellaneous bits of knowledge of fact, but is in varying degrees systematized into an organized body of knowledge. Facts are related to one another, and the entities to which they refer are thought of as constituting systems. Put somewhat differently, the situation of action, so far as men are cognitively oriented to it in this mode, constitutes an *order*. This order may be called the "order of nature."

The conception of the order of nature and its relative role in systems of action certainly varies very greatly. In the modern Western world, it has attained a stage of development not to be found elsewhere. But recent historical and anthropological investigation seems to converge on the fact that it is not only never wholly absent, but it is never a negligible factor.[32] All men, unless they are definitely "insane," are relatively well oriented to time and place. They know a good deal about the properties of their environment, its topography, climate, flora and fauna, food supply, and environmental dangers. They also know a good deal about the properties and powers of the human body, and about the characters and behavior of their fellow men.

[32] See especially Bronislaw Malinowski, *Foundations of Faith and Morals* (London: Oxford University Press, 1936.

Moreover, this knowledge is not only applied, but it is applied in ways and with attitudes which definitely show that it is not simply confused with "mystical" or supernatural ideas, although primitive people may well attribute to supernatural sources things which we would explain wholly in "naturalistic" terms. Perhaps the most impressive proof of the role of knowledge in this sense is the universal indispensability, for explanation of action, of expectations of future events and the effects of projected actions. Men universally know that the seasons will follow each other in a recognizable order, that when the sun sets in the evening, it will rise again the next morning, that when seeds are properly planted and tended, they will probably sprout and grow, etc. Such knowledge as this, examples of which could be multiplied almost indefinitely for any society, fully justifies the term "order" of nature as a part of the cognitive orientation of all human societies.

Certain writers, like Veblen, have tried to derive the scientific type of cognitive interest from some such basic human proclivity as the "instinct" of "idle curiosity." Actually, however, it is only under very sophisticated conditions that we find the pursuit of knowledge "for its own sake." The principal case of that is the professionalization of scientific pursuits, which, whatever else may be said of it, is certainly not the simple manifestation of an "instinct," but is analytically a very complex phenomenon. But in most of the simpler societies and in most situations in complex societies, the dominant case seems to be that where knowledge is primarily important in its instrumental context, it is as knowledge of the ways and means of attaining everyday practical ends that it is sought and used. That it is needed, for instance, in a ritual context does not alter this fact. The connection between astronomical knowledge of the calendar and the periodicity of ceremonies is well known.[33] But the need to fix a date for a ceremony is, once the ceremony is established as part of the life of a society, just as much a "practical" need as is the need of an adequate food supply, and the same order of considerations as to ways and means applies.

---

[33] Cf. M. P. Nilsson, *Primitive Time Reckoning* (Lund: Gleerup, 1920).

In this teleological context as well as in the predominantly cognitive, there is a further most important fact about the empirically cognitive attitude. Put in modern psychological terms, there is a universal realization and practical application of the knowledge that "wishful thinking" is out of place.[34] There is an element of fixed order of things, unaffected by wishes or affects, which, in Durkheim's term, "constrains" action.[35] The appropriate attitude is one of objective understanding, of "diagnosis," not of anger or anything else. The cases where this norm is conspicuously deviated from do not destroy, but serve to confirm, this insight.

In spite of the essentially normative ideal of positivists that it should be so, it is safe to say that human cognitive orientation is in no case *confined* to the fields of empirical knowledge, or what is measured by the standards of empirical validity and can hence, so far as it deviates from these, be dismissed as ignorance and error.[36] As in the modern case of science pursued for its own sake, there is such a thing as a predominantly cognitive interest in non-empirical problems. But equally it is safe to say that this is a very sophisticated phenomenon and is probably highly complex. As in the case of empirical knowledge, the interest in non-empirical problems seems generally to be instrumental to other contexts.

As described in terms of the action scheme, human behavior is everywhere, when seen from the point of view of the actor, teleologically oriented. It everywhere involves effort to conform with normative standards, sensitiveness to success and failure, and the phenomenon of "self-interest" in the state of the individual person, his "happiness" or lack of it. Perhaps what this is saying is merely that regarding teleological ori-

---

[34] This is not, of course, to deny that, empirically, ideas are often biased by "wishful thinking." In detail the norm of "objectivity" is widely violated, but in some form, however crude, it is universally recognized as valid, *as a norm.*

[35] Cf. Emile Durkheim, *Les Règles de la Méthode Sociologique* (Paris: Presses Universitaires de France, 1895).

[36] For a definition of these concepts see *The Structure of Social Action*, *op. cit.*, Chapter II.

entation as something more than an impersonal structure of patterns is to treat the actor as affectively bound up in the success and failure of his actions and the actions of other people.

Out of this fundamental set of facts two further points are of particular significance for present purposes. The affective orientation to normative patterns seems to involve the sense of "obligation" to conform with them. And, at least with certain of the basic patterns of this obligation, this, as an induction from experience, takes on the peculiar quality which has been referred to as "moral." This may be spoken of as the "objective" aspect of teleological orientation of action in its relation to the affective states of the actor. But, as has been said, teleological orientation to norms involves active effort; conformity does not come about "automatically," but only by "action." There is, hence, a most important element of tension as between the requirements of the normative pattern and the independent tendencies of situational development. One possible way to relieve this tension is always to abandon the normative pattern – to "let things ride" without effort. Hence, the actor has, inherently, a basic affective interest in the cognitive question of *why* he should pursue ends and conform with normative patterns. And no matter how deeply buried in the unconscious levels of personality it is, it may be said that there is always, in every human society, a process of cognitive questioning of the meaning of the moral obligations which the codes prevalent in the society impose on the individual. By the same token there is always some kind of on-going cognitive "rationalization" of these obligations. The fact that the center of attention here is upon moral obligations gives one of the fundamental starting points of the present analysis; the answers to such questions must somehow bring in what are felt to be morally authoritative sources of such obligations, sources which, however conceived, are felt to be deserving of the same order of moral respect which is enjoined toward the traditional obligations themselves.

It was said that what has just been discussed is the "objective" phase of the cognitive problems functionally related to the affective balance of the individual. Perhaps it is better to say the "disinterested" phase, because the important point is that the criteria of "validity" of a moral obligation are always dissociated from the question of whether the actor "likes" it or not; it is a matter of duty, not of preference. By contrast, the other phase may be spoken of as the "self-interested" phase. The actor becomes bound up with moral norms; they are "introjected" so that he cannot violate them without feelings of guilt or shame. But he also has "wishes" and "desires," which may be to a greater or less extent integrated with the system of moral norms he is attached to. Perhaps it can be said the he is functionally oriented to a state of "happiness" which includes above all the elements of pleasure, as defined above, and a satisfactory relation to loved persons and objects. These self-interested components of his affective orientation are, equally with the disinterested, bound up with teleological directedness. Hence the possibility of frustration is inherent in the structure of the action system. Naturally the question of "why" can occur to a reflective personality even where there is an almost perfect balance of "satisfactions" in this sense. But it becomes acute in an emotionally significant sense where there are gross frustrations of what are regarded as legitimate expectations of satisfaction.

At this point an important relation to moral obligations enters in. It is, as Durheim has shown, [37] one of the principal functions of moral norms to justify to the individual some inevitable frustrations of his self-interested wishes. But the relations of normative patterns and situation are sufficiently complex so that it often happens, not only that there are gross frustrations of what have been regarded as normal wishes, but either these frustrations are at the same time judged as morally wrong, or, perhaps an even more disturbing case, satisfactions which have been judged morally wrong and forbidden are realized on a large scale without untoward consequences to the persons enjoying them. Any of these situations gives rise to the problem of meaning as a cognitive problem in an acute form.

---

[37] Cf. Emile Durkheim, *Le Suicide* (Paris: Alcan, 1897).

What can be said about the cognitive patterns that are most closely related to these aspects of systems of action? In the first place, it is quite clear that, in no known empirical system of action, is the body of empirical knowledge, as discussed above, the dominant or principal element, though it may and does become so in accessory roles. In the first place pursuit of the question, why, in both these directions, seems by experience to lead into the realm of non-empirical considerations. The "entities," "principles," "events," etc., which "explain" these things, are usually not observable by the ordinary techniques of science. They are mythological personages and their doings, gods, demons, pantheistic principles of order, and the like. It is true that empirical observations are often involved and these need not be empirically incorrect. But they need not be interpreted in an empirically scientific context to explain *how* things happen, but may be manifestations of a source of meaning which is ordinarily non-empirical. Moreover, very generally, though perhaps not universally, these empirical objects and events may be related to each other and to the source of meaning, not by intrinsic causal relationships, but by symbolic ties. In both these respects, the cognitive structures concerned deviate widely from the type of empirical knowledge. Moreover, these deviations could be assessed by an observer who had no opportunity to observe closely the attitudes of men in asserting and discussing the propositions concerned. All he would have to know was that they were "believed."

But there is a further crucial difference on the level of attitude. Even where the attitude toward empirical phenomena is not disinterested, but very definitely interested, as in hunting food animals, the tendency is, as has been stated, toward an attitude of "objectivity" in the sense of affective neutrality. Things simply are what they are, every other consideration is irrelevant. But associated with the answers to the problem of meaning is a very definite positive affective tone; the fact which Durkheim has formulated by saying that the things talked about are "sacred" things.[38] Their sacredness consists precisely in the fact that the dominant attitude toward them is that of moral respect, or in the converse case, moral indignation. They are set apart from the utilitarian context which is dominant in the technological sphere of life, specifically insulated from being placed in an instrumental means-end context. This specific affectual attitude is related, on the one hand, to the norms of moral obligation, on the other hand, to the non-empirical entities which are conceived as the source of meaning, that is, as the ultimate terms in the current answers to the question of *why* we are obligated to do certain things and forbidden to do others, and of *why* our wishes are gratified or frustrated, as the case may be.

There is, then, current in every society, the conception of a system of non-empirical entities and forces which is specifically different from those constituting the order of nature. This cognitive structure is particularly invoked in situations in which the problem of meaning in one or both of the above senses is uppermost and is functionally related to the tensions out of which the problem of meaning arises. Moreover, it refers to entities to which the actors habitually observe an attitude directly corresponding to that of moral respect and, by virtue of this attitude, this world is "set apart" from that of "merely" empirical objects, forces, and relationships. By virtue of the non-empirical character of the more ultimate referents of this cognitive system, and of the attitude of respect, as well as because of its connection with traditional terminology, it seems justified to speak of this as the "supernatural order." It would seem that, for most purposes of the analysis of action, the situation as cognitively apprehended can be analyzed in terms of these two great cognitive "systems" and the conceptions of the relations between them. It is true that in sophisticated societies there are cognitive structures which do not obviously fit into either, such as the theory of knowledge, but they may be interpreted primarily as accessory structures developing out of the disinterested and refined pursuit of cognitive interests, and not as so basic to

[38] Cf. Emile Durkheim, *Les formes élémentaires de la vie religieuse* (Paris: Alcan, 1913), especially, Part I, Chapter III.

all systems of action in a functional way that they must play a prominent part in the most elementary analysis of action.

B. The Situation as a Field of Teleologically Directed Activity

The interrelations of the three basic modes of orientation are so close that it is in a sense "artificial" to take up any one of them in abstraction from the other two. The limitations of ordinary language in discussing theoretical questions, however, make that type of abstraction necessary. But in each case it must be remembered that they always act together, and on every relevant occasion explicit attention will, so far as possible, be called to the modes of their interaction.

A discussion of the situation as that to which the actor is teleologically oriented really presupposes logically the preceding analysis from the cognitive point of view, because the differentiation of the principal modes of teleological orientation seems to correspond to the above cognitive distinctions. The first and in certain respects analytically fundamental aspect of the situation is the fact that it is an order of nature. Corresponding to the schema of empirical knowledge, the basic schema for analysis of the teleological relation of the actor to the situation conceived as an order of nature is the "means-ends" schema. It is necessary to say a few words about the status of this schema in general by way of introduction.

The more general category within which it is placed is that of "teleological orientation." A logical necessity of the concept of teleological orientation is that there is some kind of state of affairs toward the attainment or maintenance of which action is oriented. As a general designation for this state, regardless of the kind of process involved, the term "goal" seems to be the most suitable; insofar, then, as it is teleological, action is oriented to the attainment or realization of goals. As, from the point of view of the theory of action, a limiting case, it is even possible to conceive teleological orientation as taking place without reference to any cognitive component whatever, as perhaps it is conceived in some versions of the biological concept of instinct, or that of conditioned reflex in the strict behavioristic sense.[39] Even then the concept of goal is far from meaningless, so long as there are adaptive functions in the biological sense.

But on the level of action, it is only in the limiting case that the role of cognitive orientation is negligible. Most concrete modes of teleological orientation will involve *combinations* of specific positive values of the cognitive element with the others. The "rational" or "intrinsic" means-end schema is, strictly considered, an ideal type which is conceptually defined among other things by the fact that it involves a particular limiting value of cognitive orientation: the possession by the actor of empirical knowledge which is adequate for the attainment of a clearly conceived empirical end. It seems to be the most profitable procedure here to start analytically from this rational means-end type, and to bring in other elements in terms of their deviation, at specific points, from the logical requirements of the type.

There seem to be four irreducible conceptual components of a rational "unit act" as analyzed in terms of the means-end schema: an "end;" a normative standard governing choice of means, such as, "rationality" or "efficiency;"[40] adequate knowledge of the empirical situation, that is, of the relevant aspects of the order of nature; and an affective component or the "drive," "energy," or "effort" directed to the realization of the end.

An end, for these purposes, is a subjectively anticipated future state of affairs, conceived with adequate clarity, toward which action is oriented. For purposes of the rational type, it must be an "empirical" end, that is, a state of affairs subject to empirical observation. Knowledge is

---

39 See above, p. 39 note 8, for the qualifications in use of the concept "cognitive" in the analysis of action. In general the present analysis is little concerned with the "psychological" mechanisms involved. What are sometimes, in the empirical sense of Pavlov, called "conditioned reflexes" may well, as modes of behavior influenced by experience, involve cognitive elements in the present technical and analytical sense. But this is not necessarily a sheer manifestation of "reflex chains" in the neurological sense. It is also, however, entirely conceivable that there are modes of teleologically directed behavior involving no cognitive elements whatever.

40 Irreducible for the analytically isolated unit all alone.

applied to the realization of ends very largely in the mode of prediction, or the "virtual" mode. There is, for every act, an initial situation and a future end. The actor, so far as he is in this sense rational, not only knows the present situation, but is in a position to predict its future course of development. And not only that, but he can predict its differing course of development under various hypotheses, that is assuming a series of different "ifs." Among the relevant "ifs" will be a series of alternative ways in which, by his "intervention," positive or negative, he can influence this course of development. These may include both positive intervention and deliberately refraining from doing things which are in his power to do. Some of these alternatives, his predictive knowledge will tell him will either altogether fail to lead to the "realization" of his end or will realize it only in an unacceptably inadequate degree. [41] Others he can predict will, with a certain degree of probability, adequately realize the end. Among these, according to the relevant normative standard or standards, he will "choose" the "best" or "most efficient."

Perhaps the most difficult of the components of a rational unit act to define is the normative standard of efficiency. One very important source of this difficulty lies in the fact that in concrete cases of choice or decision a very large proportion of the relevant considerations have to do with the relations of the particular unit act under analysis to others in the same system of action of the individual. Hence, it is difficult to isolate those considerations which are relevant to the analytically isolated unit act alone. Various of these systematic considerations will have to be introduced as we go along.

In its most elementary terms, efficiency clearly has reference to what may be called a "balance of advantage" to the actor. An end would not be an end, as opposed to a mere idly imagined possibility, unless its realization had a functional significance for the "welfare" of the actor, however that is to be judged. But neither would it be an end unless its realization involved effort [42] to overcome obstacles and to make neces-

41 For many ends, realization is not a matter of either/or but of degree.

42 The concept "effort" is the most difficult in the theory of action. Its role seems to be closely related [i.e. analogous – V.L.] to that of "energy" in physical systems, but it

sary decisions as to choice of means. Such future events as the coming of the next stage in the cycle of the seasons do not, however desirable to the actor they may be, constitute ends. The actor merely predicts them and adapts himself to them.

Both sides of the balance of advantage – the contribution of realization of the end to the welfare or satisfactions of the actor and the expenditure of effort – have a quantitative character, even though it is generally impossible to measure their variations in terms of a specific or constant unit. We are continually considering, in making decisions, whether the realization, or expected probability of realization, of an end is "worth" what it will "cost." On this most elementary analytical plane, cost can mean nothing but the expenditure of "action energy" or "effort." Perhaps the most important point to note is that efficiency for the theory of action cannot be measured in "physical" terms, though such things as physical product in relation to physical energy consumption of a process of action may often be important *indices* of the efficiency of the action. On the one hand, the significance of a physical result does not lie in its

---

is important to exercise care in the avoidance of reasoning by analogy. It is one of the basic facts that action is "teleologically directed." As open to subjective interpretation, this involves orientation to normative patterns. The normative pattern has reference to "states of affairs," between which and the predicted trends of the situation, there is some element of discrepancy. Action always proceeds in the *direction* of altering situational trends in conformity with normative patterns, however far it may fall short of attaining full conformity with them.

In the most formal sense, then, effort is "what makes actors swim against the current of situational trends." It is, however, possible to "locate" it, theoretically, somewhat more exactly. It cannot, analytically, itself be either an element of the situation or of a normative pattern. Neither is it, as such, an element of cognitive orientation, of knowledge, or of belief. This brings it into peculiarly close relationship to the affective aspect of the structure of the actor. This is brought out by such expressions as "he cares about … " the realization of a given goal. In a sense it may be thought of as the dynamic aspect of affect.

It should, further, be pointed out that effort has a centrally important quantitative aspect. An actor "tries hard" or "hardly tries at all." There is no constant unit in which to measure this "intensity" of effort, but comparisons of more and less are vitally important to the analysis of action.

physical properties as such, but in its functional significance to the actor as a unit in a social system; on the other hand, what is expended in attaining the result is not a physical resource alone, but "disadvantages" to the actor are incurred. Physical resources here again are important only insofar as they have functional significance to the actor as a social unit.

In terms of the above analysis, it would seem that the center of gravity of the concept of "welfare" or "balance of advantage" lies in the affective aspect of the actor's "constitution." But this fact should not be taken to imply that it is in any simple sense a matter of "hedonistic calculus." If the implications of the previous analysis are carried out here, it would appear that there are two principal aspects of this affective balance. On the one hand, the actor is integrated with a system of introjected moral norms around which his moral sentiments are organized, so that the degree of conformity with them is of positive affective significance to him. On the other hand, he has, more or less well integrated with these, a self-interested balance of "satisfactions" on the level of pleasure and of his love-hate attitudes. What is of decisive significance for the concept of the efficiency of rational action is not the balance of pleasure alone, but the bearing of the act on the total affective state of the individual.

Seen in terms of its significance for the realization of ends, the relevant part of the situation takes on the form of a set of "conditions" and of "means." It constitutes conditions insofar as its important features are not subject to the control of the actor, but must be successfully "adapted to" if the course of action is to succeed; and means insofar as it can be controlled (positively by intervention or negatively by refraining from feasible intervention) in the interest of realization of an end.

These most general features of the situation may be spoken of as technologically significant. That is, insofar as technological problems are under consideration, the situation is viewed from the point of view of its relevance to a single analytically isolated unit act with a given specific end.

Even on this "technological" level, which is analytically the most elementary, it is important to be clear how in at least two different ways elements of action other than valid empirical knowledge enter into rational action as analyzed in means-end terms.[43] On the one hand, there

---

[43] The concept of "rationality" is difficult and complex, and it is impossible in this brief essay to enter into a thorough analysis of it and its implications. There seems to be little doubt that, historically in the Western world, the primary focus of analytical attention in this connection has been valid empirical knowledge. Action is "rational" in these terms so far as it takes a course which, *given* the end, will most efficiently ensure its attainment according to knowledge of the empirical situation. To specify the concept further, it is necessary to enter into consideration of the relations of the particular unit act to others in a system. Indeed, as will be shown below, determinate analysis of the concept of efficiency implies these relations.
One of the most important aspects of the concept is the realization that, while rationality may be used as a classificatory criterion to distinguish certain types of concrete actions from others, it is not, *analytically*, adequate to determine *any* concrete type. Even the cases which are "rational" are determined by other, "non-logical" elements, other, that is, than the elements of valid empirical knowledge.
Analytically considered, rationality is a *cognitive* category and involves two elements, valid observation of empirical fact and logically clear and consistent formulation and reasoning. The former element is confined, in its relevance to action, to application to empirical situations. The latter extends to include non-empirical cognitive orientation in terms of precision of concepts and logical consistency. Though it is not, perhaps, permissible to speak of "rational" theories of the supernatural and justifications of ultimate ends, it is definitely correct to speak of rational *elements in* these theories and in the choice of ends.
The elements of "intuition" in non-empirical theories and all non-cognitive elements of action, teleological and affectual, are non-logical and as such, analytically, are neither rational nor irrational.
But in addition to its central cognitive character, the concept of rationality defines a part of the *normative* patterns governing action. It is in the nature of a normative pattern that concrete action may fail to conform to it. Lack of conformity, in turn, has two aspects, inadequate effort to realize a goal, and factors which account for the *deviation* of action from the goal, that is, for the fact that it takes the "wrong" *direction*. In this latter case, there is associated with the action a cognitive deficiency – the actor is either ignorant of relevant facts or holds erroneous beliefs about the situation. Both the above cases may legitimately be said to involve elements of "irrationality."
The question then arises of how the analysis of irrationality is to be approached. The question of the level of effort involves the affective balance and integration of the actor. It is, as will appear in the course of the analysis, never possible to speak of a

are certain conditions affecting even the ideal type form of the rational act. In the first place, the end is treated as given. To be sure there is an empirically cognitive aspect of a given end in that the actor "foresees" the state of affairs he wishes to realize. But, in addition, there is

---

concrete course of action as rational or irrational without considering the "cost" of conformity with rational norms. In these terms irrational "laziness" must mean the failure to exercise sufficient effort to achieve ends which, in terms of the actor's total orientation, it would be "worth while" for him to achieve. This may be accounted for, it seems, in one of two main directions. Either he expends a lower level of effort in this direction than in others and it is necessary to look for specific inhibiting factors. Perhaps the most common are to be found in underlying ambivalences, usually unconscious, so that a wish contrary to the manifest end blocks its "whole-hearted" pursuit. This would be a matter of relatively specific deficiencies of integration. On the other hand, it might be a matter of relatively general lack of adequate effort, which would similarly be accounted for by a conflict situation or some other aspect of lack of integration. Psychopathology seems now to accept the view that an actor's "energy" is in a sense "drained off" when he is subject to severe conflicts and repressions, by the necessity of maintaining the protective devices which relieve him of the necessity of fully "facing reality." Thus a person will often defend a belief which functions as a "rationalization" with an affective violence altogether out of proportion to the purely intellectual, or even practical, importance of the issues at stake.

The other mode of "irrationality" involves deviant tendencies. These are very generally, in a particular course of action, referable to the state of integration of the actor's personality system. But on the most general level of analysis there is a further element. It has been noted above that concrete teleological directedness involves, analytically, two distinct elements. On the one hand, there is the normative pattern element, on the other hand, the biological, which is, analytically, situational. There is no general reason why these two patterns should be exactly congruent any more than the teleological patterns generally and the non-teleological situation should be congruent. But there is a difference. The "tension" between teleological patterns generally and the non-teleological situation takes the form of "problems" of realization and of "obstacles" to the attainment of ends or the gratification of wishes. The tension between normative patterns and organic teleology, on the one hand, take the form of a conflict of different ends or of "wishes" and "obligations." This conflict is more likely to result in "irrational" conduct of the positively deviant variety in that the actor is teleologically directed to two or more incompatible goals at the same time.

This schema must, however, be used with the greatest caution. We are very prone to endow concrete wishes with the status of biological ultimacy whereas again and

the cognitive problem of "why" he should pursue that particular end rather than others. Analysis of this problem seems to lead, cognitively, in two directions. Either the particular end is important as a means to some other empirical end. Then the cognitive problem is empirical, but its consideration involves reference to the broader system of means-end relationships beyond the particular unit act. Or, on the other hand, it may be valued as an end in itself. Then its "justification" will lead into ultimate value questions and will relate this particular unit act to the whole non-empirical cognitive orientation of the actor, in particular to his conception of the "supernatural" order. It should be remembered that in both cases these considerations involve the problem of *choice* of ends. Precisely one of the principal reasons why the technological level of analysis is abstract is that an end is never just given and pursued, but it is chosen among several alternative possibilities which the situation offers. The process of choice is as fundamental to action on the level of ends as of means.

The normative standard of efficiency is apparently not on the level of system of action an independent element, but given both the aspects of affective orientation, which are significant to the level of effort, and the end, can be derived by processes of empirical cognition. This is, to be sure, true for the analytically isolated rational unit act given certain data. But concretely efficiency is, for its own sake, the object of strong clusters of sentiments which take it to a considerable extent out of the strictly rational context.

---

again analysis has shown that, even in such cases as the desire for sexual gratification, they contain important elements of "cultural" conditioning. It probably *never* occurs that the concrete conflict involved in a case of irrationality is simply a conflict between a normative obligation and a biological "wish." Freud himself, partly inadvertently, has shown the complexity of the "sexual" urge.

The most essential point here, as at so many other places in the theory of action, is the careful discrimination of analytical levels. It is doubtful whether the biological category *ever* comes directly into the problem of a psychiatrist, analyzing the origins of particular irrationalities, such as a pathological craving for alcohol, but it may well be of crucial significance on the most generalized level of the analysis of a total social system of action.

Finally, the affective balance of the actor, from which is derived the amount of effort he will expend in the pursuit of a given end, and in attempting to conform to norms of efficiency in the process, is not a matter of empirical knowledge of the situation, but must be considered as given independently of the level of knowledge. Insofar as this level of effort is subject to influence by cognitive processes at all, it appears to be much more in the direction of relation to the non-empirical aspects of cognitive orientation. The principal exception to this is the relation of the level of effort to the integration of personality in which cognitive "self-knowledge" may, as psychoanalysis has shown, play a considerable part. This will have to be discussed below. But in any case insofar as the problems of effort are subject to analysis in terms of empirical cognition, this analysis leads immediately beyond the technologically isolated unit act.

These limitations on the purely cognitive analysis of the unit act apply to the ideal-typical case of "pure rationality." It must, however, be remembered that this is a limiting case seldom attained even in a concrete unit act, probably never in a complex system of action. It has been said that it was inherent in the concept of teleologically directed action that there should be a state of tension between the affective identification with normative patterns and the tendency to the maximization of satisfactions, on the one hand, the situation and its independent tendencies of development, on the other hand. This tension would still exist even if action were purely rational. But it is notably increased by two of the actual limitations on the scope of pure rationality.

In the first place, one of the prime conditions of optimum rationality is "adequacy of knowledge." What knowledge is adequate is relative both to the end and to the concrete situation. But over a very large part of the field where the rational type is of appreciable empirical significance, this condition is in fact only very partially fulfilled. Inadequacy of knowledge impinges on action above all in that it reduces the accuracy of prediction of the effects of proposed choices of means. Strictly speaking, all predictions must be made in terms of probability; but the less adequate the knowledge, other things being equal, the lower the probability with which we can predict. Two cases will illustrate the point. In agriculture the general relations between the technological processes of preparing the soil, fertilization, planting, cultivation, on the one hand, and the quality and quantity of yield, on the other hand, are fairly well known. But in most temperate climates, at any rate, the factor of climate, notably including rainfall, temperature, and sunshine, is in the present state of knowledge highly unpredictable, but is known to influence the outcome quite largely. Hence, the outcome of planting a given field with a given crop, and caring for it in a given way, is only very approximately predictable. Secondly, in medical practice, while there is a considerable area of relative certainty of the effects of therapeutic procedures, there is an enormous area of sheer uncertainty because it is not known or only very approximately known what the effect will be.

It has been noted above that one of the very important aspects of the orientation of action to a situation is the development of a system of "expectations." This is notably true in the field of the relations between skill, effort, and the result of technological processes. The effect of inadequacy of knowledge is, given relatively stable levels of effort and skill, to frustrate definite expectations as to result. Experience shows that this added tension, which is of very considerable significance to the affective balance of welfare of the actor, has a tendency to be related to specific "non-logical" mechanisms, which have the function of reducing the tension and helping to maintain a stable relatively high level of effort. Under certain conditions magic is an important mechanism in this context; where the conditions are unfavorable to magic it is safe to assume that there is a strong tendency to the development of other types of adaptive mechanism which have a similar functional significance.

A limitation on rationality of action that is closely related to inadequacy of knowledge, but still analytically independent of it, is inadequacy of control. Knowledge is a necessary condition of control of situational processes in the context of rationality. But certain positivistic enthusiasts to the contrary notwithstanding, knowledge does not *ipso facto* yield power of control. On the contrary, the effect of an increase of knowledge is frequently to demonstrate the impossibility of certain forms of rational control, though, of course, still further advances may again open up new possibilities. Thus many primitive peoples "believe" that it is possible in some sense to control the weather, whereas it goes without saying to the modern Western mind that this is outside the range of present-day technology.

Looked at from the broadest type of "evolutionary" point of view, of course, human ends and desires must be such as are adapted to the objective possibilities of realization in the situation. But this is true only on the broadest sort of level. Similarly the body temperature of a mammal must be such as to be capable of being maintained within the range covered in the climate of its habitat. But in detail there are many discrepancies which have to be provided for by specific functional mechanisms.

To say nothing of other considerations, the functional importance to systems of action of relative stability of affective orientation, and of the corresponding expectations of satisfactions, creates a functional problem in a relatively unstable, changing situation. It would seem that the objective impossibilities of control of situations inevitably again and again impose frustrations of expectations which, however unrealistically, have come to be regarded as "legitimate." Thus, to take a prominent example, we all know in general that human beings are liable, through disease and accident, to disablement and premature death, and hence a mere reading of morbidity and mortality statistics does not in the average individual create a difficult problem of emotional adjustment. But, when it comes to his own case, or that of a person who is affectively important to him, it is another matter. Society in the modern West has built up a highly complex technology for dealing with situations of ill health. But not only is medical knowledge inadequate to meet the expectations of this situation, but there is an important class of cases where the immediate effect of the knowledge we have is to confirm the frustration, rather than alleviate it. The most conspicuous and dramatic case perhaps is that in which the physician can attain certain diagnosis of what is, on the present level of medical knowledge and technique, a certainly fatal disease. Here the effect of knowledge is to throw the inadequacy of control into even higher relief than would be the case if we were relatively more ignorant. Merely to know that one has severe abdominal pains and is disabled is one thing, to know that one has an advanced cancer of the colon with metastases is quite another. As in the case of inadequacy of knowledge, that of control accentuates the tensions between teleological orientation and situational conditions, and increases it in a way which cannot, at least immediately, be relieved again by rational techniques. Hence there is a functional need for adjusting mechanisms, the general effect of which must be in this case to stimulate a state of mind which makes the inevitable conditions at least relatively tolerable. The balance of welfare is not increased by people continually butting their heads against stone walls, but at the same time neither is it functionally "good" for a society if its actors show a craven attitude of resigned acquiescence that precludes a high level of effort. A relative delicate balance between these two dangers must be maintained, and on account of its very great functional importance is the focus of some of the most important non-logical mechanisms of action.

The discussion may now return to the rational means-end schema. So long as only the properties of the rational unit act were considered, the empirical situation was found to constitute a system of technological means and conditions of action. But it is quite clear that concretely unit acts do not occur in isolation, but as units in more complex systems of action. The complexities introduced by the organization of such units in systems throw certain further features of the situation into relief as peculiarly significant for action.

From the technological point of view, it is only in relation to the single given end that problems of the choice of means arise. But the extension of consideration to other ends in the same system introduces another "dimension." For not only are there alternative potential means to the same end, but there are also alternative uses for the same means. Either the actor must choose to which of several possible uses a means or resource shall be devoted, or if it is divisible, in what proportions it shall be distributed among the various potential uses. From the point of view of this order of choice, the technological uses and efficiencies of different means in relation to different ends are given data. As in the technological case here again choice involves reference to a normative standard which in this case may be called "economy" as distinguished from efficiency. And, finally, it also involves emphasis on a new feature of the situation, the "economic scarcity" of means.

It is true, that on the technological level, a problem of scarcity does arise. It is not merely a question of employing or not employing a resource, but often of "how much" is needed to achieve the end by a given procedure with a given degree of excellence. But since by definition no relation to other ends is admitted to consideration, the question of whether use of the means for this end will interfere with the efficient achievement of other ends, does not arise. The only element of "cost" relevant on this level is the "human" cost of effort (and probably time) which it is necessary to introduce in order to give meaning to the norm of efficiency.

Economic scarcity does not involve merely the question of whether there is "enough" for a given specific purpose, but rather exists wherever the use of a resource for one end would involve the sacrifice of its potential use for other ends and, hence, the sacrifice of the potential benefits of the alternative use or uses. The function in action of the norm of economy is, given the technological conditions of efficiency, to maximize the benefits which can be derived from a given supply of economically scarce resources or, put the other way around, to minimize economic cost, in the sense of the sacrifice of potential benefits, by allocating resources in the most "economical" way.

Economic and technological considerations are mutually interdependent but analytically distinguishable elements of rational action. They influence action in that they serve as grounds of decision in relating given situational facts to elements of the normative patterns and goals governing action. As in all cases of interdependent elements, it is meaningless to speak, concretely, of a course of action which is determined by one but not the other. This applies in particular to the "maximization" of benefits relative to the respective normative standards. Strictly speaking, it makes sense to speak of the maximization of economic benefits of "utility," or the minimization of economic cost, only under a given set of technologically relevant conditions, what some economic theorists have called the "coefficients of production." Conversely, the maximization of efficiency has meaning only on a given set of assumptions relative to the economic scarcity or "cost" of the technologically important means. In other words, efficiency has to be determined by the disadvantages, the "cost" to the actor, of carrying out a given technological procedure, and concretely the economic cost, the sacrifice of other potential utilities, is always part of this disadvantage. The distinction from the economic case lies in the fact that in the technological context we consider economic cost as given, as a constant, and only the "effort-cost" as a variable, the value of which changes as between the alternative cases which are being compared with respect to relative efficiency.

A good deal of confusion has been introduced into the discussion of these problems by using only one particular limiting case to illustrate the concept of technological efficiency, that in which economic cost is zero, or in other words where all the technologically significant means are free goods in the technical economic sense. Here, to be sure, decisions would, rationally, be reached on technological grounds "alone," as the economic element is "eliminated." But this is a limiting case of relatively slight empirical importance; concretely technological and economic elements are almost always both positively involved in decisions about the most rational choice of means. This means further that normally neither is in an "absolute" sense maximized. The rational choice of technological procedure is seldom the one which would be made if all the necessary means were economically free goods. Conversely, as is much more obvious, the rational allocation of economically scarce resources is not likely to be the same as it would be if all technological procedures could be carried out with no expenditure of effort, or even with equal expenditure.

Thus, the two sets of elements are mutually interdependent and concretely every rational choice of concrete means involves a balancing of both. Actually, however, in the "structuralization" of action systems, of which more will be said later, situations are built up where there is a relative degree of mutual "insulation" between them, so that within the sphere of functionally specialized activities and roles, it is possible within a considerable range to consider one of the two as constant and explicitly weigh only the other. Thus, in a large hospital, the doctor actually, within very broad limits, prescribes treatment which seems best for the patient on technological grounds without regard to the relative cost to the hospital or patient of the various alternatives among which the choice is made. Similarly the investment officer of an insurance company chooses among the various lines of investment open in an attempt to maximize the long-run money return from his funds, without explicitly considering the range of technological alternatives which underlie the productive process in the enterprises in which he invests. This relative "insulation" is one of the most important features of the functional differentiation of social activities and structure.

Essentially the same order of limitations on the pure rationality of action applies on the economic as on the technological level: what happens is essentially that the scope of their significance is widened. Frustrations of expectations arising from the effect of inaccurately predictable factors are significant not only for their bearing on the degree of attainment of a single end, but also in that it may mean relative loss of economic resources and thereby frustrate expectations in relation to other ends to the attainment of which those resources might have been applied.

A slightly different situation exists when it is a question of gaining control of economically significant resources. Though they are not important as ends in themselves but as means to further ends, analytically such a process of action is a technological process and subject to standards of efficiency like any other. Also, like any other, it is subject to frustrations of both kinds which have been discussed. But the consequences of the frustrations are not limited in their significance to the mere quantity of economic resources for its own sake, for instance, of money, but ramify through the whole system of ends to the realization of which those resources might potentially be applied.

The economic aspect of systems of rational action can be empirically important because of its relation to certain other features of the structure of such systems. The allocation of scarce resources is conceived by economic theory as a process of rational choice. This implies, not only that there is a plurality of ends among which to allocate the resources, but that these ends stand in determinate relations to one another. They are "weighed" in terms of their relative importance or urgency to the actor. This implies mode of relation which may be called "integration" of ends in a system. Bases of preference are not merely *ad hoc* given "urges," but are referable to more or less general matters of "principle." Indeed, along with rationality in choice of means according to efficiency, integration in terms of a coherent system of ends is one of the principal criteria of a rational system of action. Indeed, seen in its place within a system, as it always concretely exists, even a unit act can only be rational insofar as its end, and the cost of realizing it, are referable to an integrated system of ends, because this integration is logically necessary for the concrete determinacy of the concept of efficiency. The concept of an integrated system of ends is naturally a normative concept and is concretely at best approximated. Nonetheless, its role is analytically crucial to the theory of action.

Seen in the broadest terms, it is merely tautologous to say that the actor "desires" the maximum degree of realization of his total system of ends – this is true by definition. But it does not follow, except for a perfectly integrated system of ends, perfectly realized in a perfectly stable situation, that considerations of rational efficiency and economy are alone adequate to determine the teleological orientation of the actor for a particular unit act, or even for a very extensive sub-system of his action.

However much the pattern of rationality as itself a normative pattern governing action tends to affective neutrality, it must not be forgotten that all concrete action has a prominent affective component, and that this affective component is also subject to a principle of integration. The actor, then, will not consider questions of ways and means solely in terms of rational efficiency and economy, but he will have direct affective attitudes, positive or negative,[44] to the specific procedure involved in any given case.

These considerations apply to affects of all kinds. But one in particular is of crucial importance. One of the fundamental modes of affective orientation is the moral; any system of ends is directly bound up with, in large measure embodies, a system of moral values. Such a system of values consists of principles which have more or less definite "implications" for specific situations and modes of action. A system of action can, then, hardly be very highly integrated without raising the question of the "consistency" of the choice of means to particular ends with the system of values with which the ultimate ends are integrated. In detail, the considerations either of technological efficiency or of economy may

[44] As has been pointed out above, affective orientation has, basically, a polar structure. Every fundamental "positive" affect has its antithesis. This polar structure does not, however, seem to apply to an important class of cases, where, rather, an attitude of "objectivity" is called for and expected. The most notable of these is the "disinterested" pursuit of "truth" in a cognitive context, and the application of knowledge in the consideration of ways and means of attaining ends. It is this attitude of objectivity where likes and dislikes, approval or disapproval are out of place, which has been spoken of as "affective neutrality." It is exceedingly important, functionally, that affects should be, in a relative sense, excluded from certain situations. Both positive and negative affects and affective neutrality are, in the first instance, actual attitudes and not normative patterns. They are, however, to a large extent *governed* by normative patterns, so that it is *expected* that in certain situations certain affects will be manifested. These expectations are, in turn, reinforced by sanctions of approval, love, or pleasure for living up to them, disapproval, hatred, etc. for their violation. This aspect of the integration of affects with normative patterns will be further analyzed below.

well conflict with the requirements of consistent adherence to a moral code, and hence the moral quality of the acts involved presents another set of considerations relevant to questions of the choice of means. It has been customary in discussions of these problems to distinguish considerations of "expediency," what have here been called efficiency and economy taken together, from those of morality.

It is one of the primary features of integration of rational systems of action that, generally speaking and within quite broad limits, considerations of rational expediency and of moral obligation tend to correspond rather than conflict. There are three circumstances which particularly favor this correspondence. In the first place, a very large area of these considerations may touch matters relatively remote from ultimate ends, which are, of course, most closely bound up with moral values, though there is great variation from society to society in the extent of this "morally neutral area." Secondly, many value systems, particularly that dominant in the modern West, place a high valuation on efficiency and economy, as such, both for their own sakes and for the sake of their results in action. Third, a phenomenon which will have to be discussed at length below, the integration of social systems works out in such a way that it is generally to the interest of any given actor, as actually the most expedient way of attaining his ends, to conform to the common moral codes of the society, because their violation would call forth sanctions that would frustrate his activities. A very wide area of acute conflict between moral considerations and those of expediency in relation to highly urgent ends is generally to a large extent the result of the breakdown of social integration – indeed, is one of its most important symptoms and results.

What is true of moral affects is true also of the other elements of affectual orientation. All of them are, concretely, taken into account in the formulation of the concept of "cost" in both its technological and its economic aspects. For among the most important disadvantages to an actor of exerting certain kinds of effort will be the sacrifice of pleasure and of love, and the moral scruples which it may involve. Essentially the same analytical considerations apply here as were developed in analyzing the relations of technological efficiency and economy. What the introduction of the affectual elements has done is to close the circle. They had to be assumed as "constants" in defining efficiency in the first place, now they re-enter the analysis in the role of variables. Actual teleological orientation to the rational attainment of ends involves a balance, in mutual interdependence, of all these elements. None of them can be empirically isolated from the others.

It should be reiterated that the rational means-end schema formulates both a normative pattern of action and a type. In both respects it may fall short of adequately formulating a description of actual concrete action, even insofar as it is teleologically oriented. For, by definition, it fails both to include factors accounting for deviation from the rational norm and to take account of the possibilities that there may be other types than the rational, with a similar normative significance.

Factors of deviation may, it seems, be classified under two headings. On the one hand, they may be aspects of the empirically knowable situation, even though they pertain to the actor's own organism, which form part of the "resistances" to the realization of rational norms – that is, which, if altered in certain ways, would reduce the tension between normative pattern and situation. These may account for deviation in that the given level of effort may not, in view of this resistance, be sufficient to realize the end at all or in adequate degree.

On the other hand, deviation may result from a defective integration of the action system. One most important aspect of an integrated system is the freedom of its various parts from "interference" with one another. The most commonly observed aspect of the interference which is relevant here is what is usually thought of as the intrusion of irrelevant affective reactions into rational contexts where the normative pattern calls for affective neutrality. There is some doubt whether it is legitimate to call these intrusions, analytically, entirely affective. It is probable that they represent more or less integrated sub-systems of action in which the affective aspect is most conspicuous because, in analyzing the rational pattern with which they are contrasted, the chief emphasis is not on the non-affectual elements, and because the cognitive element of the intruding "complex" is outside the focus of attention. It is the affective aspect which thus is both most prominent and seems most out of place. But in general, the possibilities of malintegration of action systems, even in the case of a single actor, are almost infinitely varied. Thus, one of the main sources of the belief that men are more "irrational" than they actually are, is the fact that certain parts of the cognitive orientation of an individual may be more closely integrated with certain affective or teleological elements than with each other. Hence, a relative integration is sometimes achieved which avoids affective conflicts at the sacrifice, within certain limits, of cognitive consistency.

But above all it must not be assumed *a priori* that a given *concrete* factor of deviation from a concrete norm is of a wholly situational, for instance, biologically hereditary, character. This is, indeed, the main theoretical reason for making the distinction between the two classes of sources of deviant behavior. But it must be remembered that the distinction is an analytical one which is empirically relative. Within limits it is possible for an actor to know empirically his own modes of malintegration and take account of them rationally as conditions of his action.[45] The distinction is sharp and clear in empirical applications only on the most general analytical level, where the distinction of elements involved in the system taken as a whole is the center of attention. Concrete factors of deviation which are resistant in a particular concrete context may well contain a very large element of what are, from a more general analytical point of view, the consequences of malintegration.

The question of the role of normative types of teleological orientation other than the rational raises difficult problems. There are, in the material presented thus far, several facts which point to the theoretical possibility of such types, probably more than one. It has already been

[45] This limit, however defined in specific terms, is very important as one criterion of the distinction between "normal" and "pathological" behavior. A person's action is pathological, e.g., "neurotic," when he is influenced by conflicts into the nature and importance of which he has defective insight.

seen that the "justification" of ultimate empirical ends leads into non-empirical considerations, involving the actor's orientation to a supernatural order. Given the fact that non-empirical "reality" is a significant part of the situation, there is the theoretical possibility that ends themselves should be, wholly or partly, non-empirical states of affairs and yet play a significant role in action. Thus to give one of the simplest possible examples, the span of an individual human life is known to be rather definitely limited and yet we find action oriented to states of affairs of the individual as a distinct entity which he knows cannot apply to the time of his organic life, but only to what happens to him in the "after life." Such a time location of ends is for our analytical purposes non-empirical. But it is not only in the time dimension that the existential reference of ends can "transcend" the limits of empirical experience.

Where this situation is present, the question arises of linking up the transcendental elements of the end with the empirical situation in which a choice of means must take place. No very extensive analytical problems appear to be involved here. What can be said is that the way this is done depends on the cognitive theory the actor holds as to the relation between his non-empirical end and the empirical situation in which he is placed. Thus, Calvinistic theology provides an elaborate account of the content of the will of God, and is hence capable of orienting the believer to the empirical modes of action, and the more immediate empirical ends, which are "pleasing in the sight of God." This is a particularly good case, because the *only* non-empirical elements admitted are the conception of the ultimate transcendental end of man's existence, the performance of God's will, and the account of the content of that will, which defines the empirical ends of action. But with the exception of a few rituals regarded as directly ordained of God, all concrete action is held up, so far as possible, to the pattern of intrinsic rationality.

But this case, which is the most closely assimilated to the rational pattern, by no means exhausts the possibilities. Elements of the empirical situation, even though cognitively known in the same way as in the empirical means-end pattern, may have a different significance. They may, that is, be linked symbolically, on the one hand, to affective states of the individual, on the other hand, to non-empirical entities, particularly supernatural.

C. The Situation as Object of Affective Orientation: Cathexis

This presupposes another aspect of the situation, not yet dealt with. Affective orientation involves, not a merely subjective state, but a mode of *relation to objects* which, using the Freudian term, may be called "cathexis." What has been called "affective neutrality" is a limiting case, and it is dubious whether its significance is merely negative. But situational objects are, in addition to being observed and known, objects of love and hate, of desire and aversion, and many other nuances of emotion.

In relation to their affective significance to the actor, situational objects may be direct objects of affects, "for their own sake." This is true of persons we love or hate, of a prized picture or anything of the sort. Or, on the other hand, the affective significance may not be direct, because the affective attitude is appropriate to the object itself, but indirect, because it has associations with an affectively significant object. If the associations were simply those of empirical cause and effect, the analysis would fit into the patterns already discussed. But there is another possibility, namely, that the association should be such that the object has a symbolic relation to the source of its affective significance. There are doubtless many possible variations among the sub-types of such symbolic relations which cannot be gone into here. But they have in common the fact that they cannot be fitted in as intrinsically rational means to an empirical end.

It is possible for affects to enter into teleologically oriented action only insofar as they supply a motive for the desirability of attainment of the end. Indeed, according to the previous analysis, it is the intensity of affect which supplies the source of "effort," the motive force for caring whether an end is attained or not. But in the pure type of rational action the choice of means is conceived as affectively neutral. This may not be the case.

The actual acts, as well as the accompanying linguistic expressions, may have symbolic significance as expressions both of affective attitudes and of teleological orientations to goals of various sorts. Even on a relatively unorganized level, there is an element of normative regulation here in that not any old symbol will do to express a given attitude, but there is a certain "appropriateness," referable to resemblances, past associations, or something of the sort.

To a widely varying degree, such expressional symbols are organized in systems. Insofar as this is on the whole abstracted from an actively teleological context, they form such structures as artistic "styles." But there seems also to be a well-defined tendency to consider the manipulation of appropriate symbols as a *means* of teleological orientation to particular goals, even goals which may be sufficiently clearly conceived to be considered ends.

This integration of symbolically significant acts in teleologically oriented structures may conceivably take place regardless of the character of the symbols. But one of the most important types is that where there is a symbolic relation to supernatural entities and, hence, the symbolic act is performed with the specific attitude of respect for sacred things. This is the case which it seems convenient to call "ritual" action, which is of very great empirical importance.

In concrete cases of ritual, there is, to varying degrees, an explicitly conscious linking up of the specific symbolic acts with clearly conceived goals or ends in the role of means. But in any case there is a definite normative element in the action. The things are nor merely "done," but it is *obligatory* that they should be done, and done in the specifically prescribed ways. If asked why this obligation exists the actor may be able to say no more than that it does exist and somehow must or the ancestors have so ordained it. From this pole there are found all degrees of rationalization, from what are rather obviously *ad hoc* inventions, perpetuated perhaps by tradition, which give a mere veil of plausibility, to the case where the act is clearly essential to the acting out of a highly rational theory of the attainment of transcendental (or empirical) ends through the manipulation of supernatural forces. [46]

In some sense or other, the performer of a ritual act can always be said to "believe" that it is "useful" or "reasonable" to do what he is doing and, the more highly rationalized the case is in the above sense, that it is necessary to the attainment of some end. In this "rational" statement, the linguistic justification of the action takes a form which is readily comparable with the empirically rational explanation of why certain choices of means are efficacious in bringing about certain ends. Hence, the strong temptation to judge the action by the standards of empirical rationality. Of course, judged by these standards, the act turns out to be "irrational" since there is no adequate scientific evidence that doing these things has any influence on the desired result, or in the case of empirical ends, there is often positive evidence that they do not.

But it is dangerous to accept this "belief" as too naively the equivalent of the modern Westerner's belief in the propositions of empirical knowledge. In one of the most prominent types of cases of ritual action, the magic prevalent in primitive societies, it is a striking and adequately established fact that the participant does not, typically, *confuse* the magical procedure with the rational technique which always runs parallel with it. His "error" is only one, the negative, aspect of his action. There is a positive significance in addition, which is capable of analysis in terms of the symbolic significance of the component acts and properties, and linguistic expressions, both in relation to the affective and teleological orientations of the actor, and in relation to his conception of the supernatural order, and of the functional relation of all these things to the system of action. This can be said to have been proved beyond all reasonable doubt. [47]

---

46 An excellent example of this type is the Catholic mass.

47 See, especially, Bronislaw Malinowski, *Coral Gardens and Their Magic* (London: Allen and Unwin, 1935), volume I.

D. The Situation as Social: The Other Actors

So far nothing explicit has been said about one crucially important fact about the situation in which any given actor acts – the fact that it contains other human individuals. This could have been taken up under each of the three aspects of the significance of the situation to action, but its implications in all three respects are so closely interwoven that it seems better to treat them all together in a separate section.

On the cognitive level, no peculiar analytical problems seem to be raised. Other human beings are known in the first place as empirical objects, which, whatever their affective significance, differ as objects of cognition from others only in that knowledge of them involves different frames of reference, and that the cognitive problems are, if anything, more complex and difficult. Whether there is non-empirical knowledge of other individuals remains for present purposes an open question. It can be said that none has successfully been integrated for analytical purposes with the theory of action. This is *not*, however, to say that the non-empirical ideas which are current relative to the nature, or significance with reference to value, either of human beings generally or specific individuals, such as, prophets, are unimportant. They are to be dealt with in the same way as other non-empirical ideas. But on both the teleological and the affective levels, there are very important problems specific to this aspect of the situation.

It is perhaps best to begin again with the rational means-end schema, as it is possible to formulate the relationships more precisely for this limiting case and then introduce the qualifications for departures from it. Since other individuals are parts of the empirical situation, they are, from the point of view of a given actor, potentially significant to his action in the role of conditions or of means. But they have what are, in this context, certain fundamentally significant properties which are entirely lacking in inanimate objects, and much less significant in animals. They are themselves actors in a social system. They are themselves oriented to the action of the individual of first reference, and they "respond" to his actions and prospective actions in terms of their bearing on their own action-system.

Seen in terms of the teleological significance of this fact to a given actor, he needs knowledge of what other actors do, and are likely to do, in order that he may use his control over them to induce them to do what he wants, as a means to his own ends, or to prevent them from doing things which would be detrimental to the achievement of his ends. Or, insofar as he cannot control their action, they constitute elements of the conditions of the situation to which he must adapt himself.

A double question then arises: first, of the various possible ways in which it is possible for him, as a means to his ends, to attempt deliberately to influence the action of others; second, reciprocally, of the ways in which others may attempt to influence his action and hence which he must be prepared to meet. It will simplify the exposition if the actor who is exerting influence on the other in the service of his ends is called A, while the object of his efforts is called B. A will, for this discussion, be assumed always to be acting rationally, while one of the most important possibilities is that he should take advantage of the limitations of B's rationality, or of B's non-logical sentiments.

Adequate knowledge is one of the most important conditions of rationality of action. It is conceivable that A should possess knowledge which, if B possessed it, would be significant to his action and on the basis of which he would alter his otherwise projected course. A may then seek to influence B, either positively to do something he wants done or negatively to forestall something he wants to prevent, by imparting this information to B, and letting him "draw his own conclusions," that is, proceed in pursuit of his own ends on the basis of the new "definition of the situation." This method may be called "enlightenment." An example is the purely informative aspect of advertising. Its antithesis is the case where A, fearing something B might decide to do if he possessed the information, or that he would refrain from carrying out what is to him a desirable intention, deliberately withholds the information in order to influence B. Thus A, a businessman, knows that his business is insolvent, but withholds the information from his creditors to prevent them from instituting bankruptcy proceedings.

Closely related to the latter case is that of “misinformation” where A, in order to get B to do what he wants or prevent him from doing something, positively misinforms him as to the relevant state of affairs. In this field there is a series of different types shading into each other: withholding of information may vary from merely failing to take an unusual initiative in enlightening B, to deliberately withholding information which A knows is important to B and that B has a “right” to know. Misinforming may vary from merely allowing B to continue to hold an erroneous belief with the origin of which A has had nothing to do, to the case where A deliberately inculcates such a belief when B obviously would not have arrived at it independently of his influence. The term “fraud” in general usage connotes influencing action by either misinformation or failure to inform when it is considered ethically unjustified to do so. The significance of attitudes of ethical justification will appear in the course of the analysis. For most purposes it is convenient to speak of influencing action through control of information as such, as varying between the poles of enlightenment and fraud.

But further, given that both A and B are in possession of the relevant facts of the situation, A can attempt to get B to do, or refrain from doing, something, as he wishes, by offering, contingent on B’s performance, to use some aspect of his control over the relevant situation, to alter it in a direction which he, knowing B’s ends, knows would be to B’s advantage. We would, in common speech, find it appropriate to describe this as “buying” B’s assistance, and it is, in fact, the type case of economic exchange. The channel of influence here is neither through B’s ends nor his knowledge, but through the situation itself, given both knowledge and the ends. This also has a corresponding negative case. A may, that is, seek to prevent B from doing something he would probably otherwise do which he, A, does not wish to happen; or to get him to do what he otherwise would not, by threatening, contingent on B’s failing to perform, to use his, A’s, control over the situation in some way to alter it to B's disadvantage. This case may be called "coercion." The line between exchange and coercion is analytically definite, but empirically, specific things may fall on one side or the other according to the context, particularly the time span considered and the extensity of the system of unit acts under consideration. In the present context force is significant as one among many possible instruments of coercion insofar as A is in a position to exercise force over B. But it is significant that here it enters in only as the *threat* of force, leaving the alternative of having it actually applied, or as between two different applications, open to B.

From B's point of view, submission to coercion takes the form of exchange. Given A's threat to alter B's situation to his disadvantage, B "buys him off" by meeting his conditions, which avoids the sanctions. But where coercion is present on one side, the relation of exchange cannot be reciprocal, whereas in "economic" exchange it always is. But reciprocity, or "mutual advantage" in exchange, does not presuppose equality of advantage or of "bargaining power."

Closely related to coercion, but distinguishable from it, is "compulsion." Here B is left no alternative, but something, which he does not desire, is "done to" him. The aim of compulsion, from A's point of view*, is necessarily negative, to *prevent* B from doing something he does not want done.[48] The means of compulsion, as of coercion, are various. Thus a summary dismissal of an employee is compulsion. But physical compulsion is one of the mot important of these means.

Indeed the importance of the role of force in human affairs derives in the first instance from the fundamental fact that the actor is an entity of which, concretely, another aspect is a living biological organism. His ability to act and the attainment of many or most of his ends are contingent on the state of the organism, its freedom from spatial confinement, its state of health, and its continuing to live. Hence, whoever, by physical force, is in a position to interfere with any of these essential

* Marginal note in Parsons' hand at this point on his personal copy "can be vindictive" – V.L.

48 It may, of course, have other functions than the influencing of B's future action, e.g., "punishment" for past acts.

conditions of action can exert an enormous influence on the action of others. The fact that the organism must, at any given time, have a specific location in space is of crucial significance for the organization of social relationships through its relation to the territorial principle. As a principle of authority, this depends for its peculiar significance on the fact that human beings are subject to the use of force for physical coercion and compulsion. These matters will be discussed more fully below when the modes of "structuralization" of action systems are taken up.

The enlightenment-fraud type of influence and the exchange-coercion type both assume, not only that B acts rationally within the limits relevant to the analysis, but that A makes no attempt to influence his ends, leaving him to pursue them in the light of the situation itself and of his knowledge of it. But without going into the limitations on B's rationality, there is the further possibility that an attempt may be made to influence B's ends. This may be done by attempting, rationally so far as possible, to "persuade" B that he should act as A desires him to by accepting the ends A wants him to pursue. There are a number of possible ways in which A may attempt to persuade in this sense and still remain within the bounds of a relative rationality. Most people would probably think at once of the difference between appealing to B's "self-interest" and to his sense of "duty." While significant for certain purposes, this distinction is probably less so than is usually thought, and will not be emphasized here. Perhaps the most clearly rational type of case is that in which A appeals to the integration of B's system of ends. That is, he argues that B's proposed end is less in harmony with what B "really" wants to achieve than is the end A proposes that B should substitute for it. A common case of this type of persuasion would be the giving of advice on choice of a career where, from a broader perspective, an older man tried to show a younger that an alternative would come nearer realizing the more fundamental desires and values of the younger than the choice he had first thought of. Indeed, what is commonly spoken of as the giving of "advice," where it does not constitute enlightenment, usually falls, in ideal type, under the heading of persuasion. It may, however, shade over imperceptibly into the types where A takes advantage of the limitations of B's rationality, consciously or unconsciously.

The strict case of rationality would seem to be limited to the placing of the alternative ends in question in the broader context of B's total system of ends, of helping him, that is, to integrate his action. But the more this leads to the reconsideration of the status of B's more ultimate ends and value-orientation, the more it shades over into another type which, instead of persuasion, may be called "conversion." Conversion may, however, have the element in common with persuasion that A attempts to influence B by rational argument. But it may be stated, as a tentative generalization, that the more it becomes a question of the basic value-orientation, the less it is likely that rational argument on the cognitive level plays the predominant role. [49]

Underlying the distinctions between enlightenment and fraud, between exchange and coercion, there is a question of A's broader "intentions" toward B. While there is by no means an immediate and direct correspondence in all cases, there is a general tendency for enlightenment, exchange, and persuasion to be connected with "favorable" or "friendly" general attitudes toward B, while fraud and coercion tend to be associated with hostile attitudes. Of the three types of method of influence resting on the assumption of B's rationality, persuasion is that where the rational basis is perhaps most precarious. There seems to be no important basis of difference in technique as a function of A's intentions, but in the empirical implications for the stability of social systems, there is a very important difference. On the one hand, A may attempt to persuade B, either for B's own "good" or in furtherance of a value system which may be reasonably imputed to B and of which A approves. Or, on the other hand, A may act to injure or destroy B, or to persuade him to accept ends which belong in a value system of which A does not approve, and the realization of which he wishes to prevent. Since A's intentions toward B are, from the latter's point of view, an important part

[49] Especially in a particular individual case. The role of "reason" may be very different in determining the differentiation of movements of conversion.

of the situation in which he acts, this latter case, if persuasion is to be effective, involves concretely, an element of fraud on A's part, since if B knew that A's intentions were hostile, he would probably not be open to persuasion.

It has been shown above that only in a limiting case is an actor's attitude to a specific end, or the choice of means to it, ever purely a matter of expediency. There is always some mode of the relation of considerations of expediency to those involved in moral attitudes. In its application to the modes of influencing the actions of others, this fact leads to the analytical basis of one of the most important phenomena of social systems. That is, either in whole or in part, B may, insofar as he is aware that A is trying to influence his action, recognize that A has a "right" to do so, that what he is doing is, in terms of B's own moral values, "legitimate." The conception that there should be such a thing as a right to influence the action of others carries with it the implication of its negative, there will be modes and spheres in which B considers it illegitimate for A to try to exercise whatever potential control he may possess in fact. But, on the positive side, there is a distinction between two types of permissible or legitimate exercise of influence. On the one hand, A may have a merely permissive right, what may, following Dean Pound, * be called a "liberty" to attempt to influence B in certain ways. What this means is that there is no moral ground for B forbidding A to do this. On the other hand, however, there may be a positive right in that, in doing so, A is performing what B recognizes to be a positively valuable function in terms of the value system which B himself recognizes as valid. In this case, it may be said that A exercises "authority" over B. Mere ability to influence the action of another, regardless of moral considerations, may be called "power."

The concept of power has meaning where the other individuals are treated as simply affectively neutral elements of the situation of A's

---

* Roscoe Pound, long-term Dean of the Harvard Law School at the time Parsons was writing and author of *The Spirit of the Common Law* (Boston: Marshall Jones Company, 1925), a work that Parsons admired – V.L.

action. But the distinction of the three different modes of exercise of power, illegitimate use, liberties, and authority, brings in another element. Not only is this an affective element, but it refers to a mode of integration of individuals with one another in social systems. For authority can only exist where, in some sense, the action of A is subsumed under B's system of moral values. It is still, however, logically possible that A should not recognize those values – should, that is, in a sense be perpetrating a fraud on B. The whole problem of integration on the affectual, including the moral, level raises important functional questions which will be approached below.

In the narrower sense "rationality" is limited to considerations of empirical knowledge. Hence, in respect of ends, its role, as a mode of influence, is limited to questions of empirical fact and of logic. Where it comes to the question of the status of ultimate ends, non-rational elements enter in. But a cognitive mode of orientation that is as closely as possible assimilated to empirical knowledge may be predominant in one limiting type. That is, as has been pointed out, the attempt to "convert" may be carried out as far as possible by rational argument, by trying to show B what the non-empirical situation "really is." An excellent example of this is to be found in the philosophical discussions of the Upanishads, where the Brahman intellectuals tried as far as possible to keep their religious orientations on a cognitive level.

But from this pole, conversion varies to the type where a fundamental value-orientation is held up in non-cognitive, or even self-consciously anti-intellectualist, terms. The slogan, *credo quia absurdum est,* expresses the limiting case in this direction. The main line of early Christianity may be said, however, to be mainly non-cognitive in emphasis, neither intellectual, as was the case in the Indian religions of salvation, [50] nor anti-intellectual, as tends to be the case, for instance, with National Socialism.

It is, of course, very unlikely that a classification like the present one would exhaust all the possibilities of such a field, and no such claim

---

[50] See Max Weber, *Gesammelte Aufsätze zur Religionssoziologie*, (*op. cit.*) volume II.

is made. It is, however, necessary to consider one more type. A may attempt to influence B, without pretending to touch his ultimate value-orientation, by playing on his non-logical and irrational "sentiments," regardless of, or in contrast to, normative considerations. This mode of influence may most conveniently be called "propaganda." It is by no means out of the question that purely non-rational mechanisms, not capable of subjective understanding at all, should be played upon. But, insofar as it is a question of phenomena on the level accessible to the theory of action, affects will tend to play a prominent part, and also systems of symbolically significant associations, often primarily on the affective rather than the cognitive level. A typical propaganda technique, very frequently observable in advertising, is for A to attempt to create a favorable attitude toward something, such as a product, by associating it with something to which B is likely to have a favorable attitude already. Thus, in relation to health, such a vague phrase as "doctors recommend ... " may have such an effect in that people very generally have a favorable attitude toward the medical profession. Here, of course, the appeal would not be rational unless either the specific medical reasons why the product was recommended were given, and the reader of the advertisement were capable of understanding them, or the specific medical authorities and just what they had said were quoted in a verifiable manner. Here the very fact that medical ethics prevents reputable doctors from giving testimonials opens the door to vague appeals which readily exploit the generally favorable attitude toward the profession. A rather extreme type of propaganda appeal is printing a picture of a pretty girl in an advertisement, where the picture has nothing whatever to do with the technical qualities of the product (a toothpaste, for instance), in order to create favorable attitudes simply by the fact that people, particularly men, like to look at such a picture, and being thereby put in a genial mood are less critical toward the produce advertised.

The fact that propaganda in this sense "works" is not to be taken to mean that human beings are moved by "brute instincts" or something of the sort, but is rather an index of the complexity of the systems of action of modern society, and hence of the difficulty of their full integration. Where what is touched is a system of symbolic associations, very often it is association with the patterns of normative significance, with moral sentiments and the like, which is the main basis of the appeal. The opportunity for propaganda lies, not in the fact, either, that it is antisocial impulses which are appealed to, but that the authenticity of the connection between the normative pattern and the particular thing or act is not sufficiently critically thought out on a rational level.

Of course, propaganda does not always appeal primarily to the socially desirable normative patterns. It appeals also to all sorts of sentiments that may be petty, envious, aggressive, or hostile. The theory of psychopathology has given us a great deal of insight into the mechanisms which make this possible. In any society, by virtue of the mere fact that there are necessarily large-scale frustrations of legitimate expectations, and the more disorganized the society, the more conspicuously, there is a great mass of "aggression" and hostile sentiment. Precisely because much of this is in conflict with the dominant normative patterns and because, functionally, its free expression would be dangerous to the stability of the social system, much of it is repressed. But, as Freud has shown us, repressed material has symbolic associations with elements on the level of consciousness. Thus, by playing on the proper symbols, it is possible for propaganda to activate repressed aggressive sentiments and this is a phenomenon, particularly today, of the greatest empirical significance.[51]

Before taking up the corresponding cases where not only B but A departs from the norm of rationality, a few words need to be said more explicitly about the affective significance of other individuals in the situation. The potential action of B may be, to A, a possible source of pleasure or displeasure. Pleasure and its polar antithesis, being subjective manifestations of organic states, cannot, in a certain sense, be "shared," but are wholly private to the individual. This is true in spite of the fact

[51] To give only one example: the success of anti-Semitic propaganda is largely explicable in terms of this sort.

that a person can very well take pleasure in someone else's pleasure and, conversely, feel another's suffering as positively painful. On this account it would appear that other individuals, as sources of pleasure and displeasure, fit mainly into the teleological rather than the affective context. It is only when the relation to another individual is affectively significant through love-hate and moral elements that B is treated in terms other than teleological expediency, and because of and through these other affective elements.

With respect to the love-hate dimension of affective orientation, on the other hand, it is certain that other individuals are among the most significant, if not *the* most significant, of the possible objects of such attitudes. This is particularly true because of the fact, pointed out above, that this mode of affectual orientation is "cathected" to individual objects as such. The thing which apparently gives the special significance to human individuals as such objects is the reciprocal character of the relation, the fact that B may "respond" to A's love or hate. It makes sense to say that one "loves" a painting or symphony, but not to say, conversely, that the painting loves its human admirer. But with human beings, to a less extent with animals, the response is of the first importance.

One of the most important aspects of the bearing of such affective attitudes on action is the fact that among the most important goals or ends of individuals is the securing of desired modes of response from others, or the avoidance of undesired ones. It is further true that the affective significance of individuals is involved in complexes of symbolic relationships, just as is true of other affectively significant things. Hence, any mode of action which tends to activate symbolic associations can, in intricate ways, be intertwined with the symbolic complexes in which affectively significant individuals play a part. Persons may have symbolic significance, conscious or unconscious, in relation to other significant things, empirical objects or normative patterns, or, vice versa, these other things may be symbolically associated with affectively significant persons.

The role of other individuals in the context of moral attitudes is nonetheless significant. It is true that moral attitudes are not focused on persons as such, but on abstract ideal patterns. However, the actions and qualities of persons are perhaps the most important concrete things to which moral judgments are applied. Here, the fundamental reciprocity of relations between persons comes in, in a fundamental role. A cannot only love or hate B, he can approve or disapprove of him and of what he does; he stands, positively, in the role of lending "recognition" to B. But this relation is reciprocal. A is also a potential object of the moral attitudes of B. Notably he may desire his approval and fear his disapproval. This will certainly be true so far as the two are "integrated" in their moral attitudes, so far as they approve and disapprove the same things. The only important qualification of this is that made necessary by the differentiation of roles, where, though the two are subject to common standards insofar as they are expected to do the same things, they are, in fact, expected, within important limits, to act differently.

The object of moral approval is, as a person, typically the object of the attitude of respect. The relation between a personal object of respect and a moral code is reciprocal. It would appear that, analytically, the approval of principles is prior, that of persons secondary through "application." But concretely very often the attitude to the person is better defined than to the code. Then, whatever that person does tends to be approved because *he* is respected – "a good tree cannot bear evil fruit." This phenomenon is probably associated with the importance of human individuals as objects of love as well as moral approval. Especially when the two components are well integrated the centering of attitudes of moral respect on persons strongly backs up the authority of principles. But, with malintegration, this is also a source of cumulative undermining of principles and codes, in that a person who is respected may do things in violation of the relevant code. The fact that he is respected puts those who respect him in a conflicted situation. One way to mitigate the intensity of the conflict is to withdraw at least part of the intensity of the moral feeling from the code: "if *he* does it, it can't be so bad after all."

But perhaps the most important case of the moral influence of persons is that of adults, particularly parents, on children. For the child is systematically trained to observe an attitude of respect for his parents long before he is mature enough to grasp the meaning of the moral codes the parent upholds and inculcates. In fact, what is built up is, in the above sense, a position of authority for the parent, which in turn legitimizes to the child the particular rules and principles of smaller scope which are inculcated. Only at a relatively late stage is there an adherence to codes, like "fairness," as such, regardless of personal agents.[52] In view of this situation, it is comprehensible why imperfect moral integration and consistency on the part of parents can have a particularly disastrous influence on the children.

It has already been pointed out that strong affective attitudes of either type seldom exist without an important degree of integration with teleological orientation. Thus generally speaking we wish to possess or control things which give us pleasure, to avoid or even destroy things which are hedonically negative. We tend to further the interests of persons we "love," to care for them, to "identify" ourselves or our interests with them, while we tend to be hostile and aggressive toward persons we "hate," to obstruct them, even, in the extreme case, to destroy them. Finally, we tend to want to associate with people we approve morally or in another slightly different sense to "identify" ourselves with them, while we tend to avoid those of whom we disapprove, in the extreme case, especially if they interfere with us, to combat them actively. These positive tendencies are particularly derived from the significance to each individual of the effects on him of the reciprocal character of affective orientation, of the subjective significance to him of "response" and "recognition" which Thomas, quite rightly, specifies as two of the really fundamental "wishes" of the human social individual. Conversely, hostile and disapproving attitudes, precisely because their objects desire

52 See the works of Jean Piaget.

and need the contrary, tend to arouse reciprocal hostilities and disapprovals, which tend both cumulatively to intensify the affects, thus to intensify the teleological impulses, and in turn to arouse still more intense reactions on the other side.

In view of the importance of other persons on the affectual level, and of the close integration of this with teleological orientations, it would be surprising if there were not modes of attempting to influence the actions of others which fall outside the rational schema. Indeed, exactly the same considerations apply here as apply to teleological orientation generally. There are probably various normative modes other than the empirically rational. One is certainly the ritual mode. Most, at least, of the types of exerting influence which have been distinguished for the rational case would seem to have their ritual counterparts. Thus there may be ritual enlightenment in the form of imparting ritual formulas; there may be exchange of such "goods;" there may be ritual coercion, even, as is fully attested, ritual compulsion, [53] etc.

Even in the rational case, naturally, concrete action, which is never fully rational, often has unanticipated consequences, some of which are important to the actor. But, generally speaking, in relation to natural phenomena, such as, the weather, the striking thing to the Western mind about magic is the persistent belief in it in spite of the fact that it has *no* important objective effect. But where the object of control is human, this is by no means so likely to be the case. Where, for instance, war magic is performed and where, as is often the case, the enemy both knows it is and believes in the efficacy of magic, it is quite possible that he may be afraid of the effect of it and actually fight less vigorously because of that fear. Or, a still better established case, where ritual methods of healing are employed, there is every reason to believe that the ritual importantly affects the state of mind of the "patient" and, through this, his state of "health," especially in certain types of cases, so that it may actually cure him or contribute to his cure. Indeed, in some cases we are in a position

---

53 In the extreme case, a person may be killed by black magic. Cf. Reo F. Fortune, *The Sorcerers of Dobu* (London: Routledge, 1932).

to understand, more or less adequately, the actual mechanisms, usually of a "psychological" character, by which this takes place.

Here the mechanisms of effect may be accessible to empirical understanding. But two things must be said. In the first place, the actor himself is generally not in possession of this knowledge. If he were, he probably would act differently. But, secondly, his mode of normative orientation is different from the rational. So far as this is true, in a sense, such knowledge is irrelevant.

Generally speaking the bearing of these considerations on the main line of analysis seems to be the following: the importance of propaganda and conversion as rational modes of action on A's part shows the possibilities of influencing B by "non-logical" means, from A's point of view. But A need not be acting rationally in this sense. Insofar as he is not, but is acting ritually, for instance, his acts may still have an effect on B through these non-logical mechanisms. These effects may be in line with A's own teleological intentions: A as a Navajo "singer" may cure B, his patient, of an actual illness; or A as a religious prophet may convert B to his sect. Or, on the other hand, the effect may be something other than what A intends, in which case it is not best treated as "error" in the ordinary sense of violation of a norm of rationality. The main point is that there is an immense amount of reciprocal influencing of individuals by each other which is empirically real, and of great importance in its effects, but is not susceptible of analysis in terms of the rational means-end schema. It is accessible nonetheless through others of the subjective categories of the theory of action. Above all the concrete phenomena that fit in this picture, such as, magic and the mass movements of non-logical religious conversion, should not be treated *merely* as significant "manifestations" of the states of mind of the actors. They are that. But each treatment tends to imply that they are without important influence on real action, particularly on that of other individuals. This is by no means the case. They are *also* modes of very real influence of the actors concerned on other individuals in the same social systems.

IV. Some Functional Needs of Social Systems

The ground has now been laid for taking up, at least in certain aspects, the problem of the functional necessities of a social system as a whole, as distinguished from the individual actor. Of course, concretely, as will be developed in outline later, individual functional needs are typically met through more or less complicated modes of social organization with differentiation of roles and the resulting functional interdependence of actors on various levels. Thus no individual normally feeds or clothes himself from start to finish.

But the functional necessities of the social system as a unit are of a different order. The most conspicuous is that of "stability." In some sense, a social system tends to "stable equilibrium,"[54] to the maintenance of itself as a "going concern" *as* a system, and the maintenance of some kind of a structural pattern, either stably or through a course of development. In this respect it is analogous (*not* identical) to the organism and its tendency to maintain, from a short-time point of view, a physiological equilibrium or "homeostasis" and, from a longer-run point of view, the curve of the life cycle.

Stability in this sense is only possible if there is some significant degree of "integration" of the various component parts of the system, in this case the individual actors. Further, integration, in the relevant sense is a matter of the *relations* of the actors, including the modes in which they influence each other. An analysis of the various possible modes of mutual influence, such as that just carried out, is thus part of the necessary logical prerequisite of a consideration of the problem of integration of social systems.

The application of this analysis to the problem of integration consists in raising the question: what would be the effect on the stability

---

54 Cf. Vilfredo Pareto, *Traité de Sociologie Générale* (Paris: Payot, 1917-19), Chapter XII. See also, L. J. Henderson, *Pareto's General Sociology* (Cambridge: Harvard University Press, 1935).

of social systems if one, a considerable number, or all of the component actors, persistently and intensely, attempt to influence the action of others in each of the different ways.[55] Reflection will show that, on the simplest analytical plane, there is nothing inherently opposed to stability in the attempt to enlighten people, to induce reactions by free offers of economic exchange, by rational persuasion, or by certain types of non-logical attempt to influence, including ritual healing, "white" magic generally, and the common participation in the same religious rituals.

Something is similarly true on the affective level. If two people have been so conditioned to each other that the presence or probable actions of each is likely to give the other pleasure, their relations are on the whole likely to promote the stability of the social system. The same is true if their personal affectual attitudes are positive, if they "love" one another, are "fond" of or "friendly" to each other, etc., equally if they morally approve and respect one another's qualities and actions.

In both the teleological and the affective cases, it can be said that concrete exceptions to the integrating effect of such modes of influence can be accounted for in terms of the lack of perfect integration of the system of action, both personal and social, in which they occur. Thus, for a poorly adjusted individual, to have information withheld from him may well, in a concrete case, promote his effective functioning as a social unit. It is often necessary, in order to prevent antisocial actions, to exercise compulsion or coercion on individuals. It is even favorable to the social system if some individuals, whose action does not conform to its functional requirements, are hated or morally disapproved.

With certain of the other modes of mutual influence, however, the

---

55 This is not, however, the only aspect of the problem of stability or "order." It is possible for two actors, whose action is in the first instance not oriented to each other at all, to come into relation and perhaps conflict. Thus, though their ends are quite lacking in integration, positively or negatively, they may both seek control of the same scarce means, which, as Hobbes put it, they "both desire but nevertheless cannot both enjoy." But in this case their action does become mutually oriented and susceptible of analysis in such terms. Hence, the discussion will be confined to the problem of mutual influence.

situation is different. Thus, of the rational types of exercising influence, it is evident that fraud, coercion, compulsion, and propaganda are readily susceptible of being used by A to injure B, or to promote A's interests at the expense of B. This may result in depriving the social system of B's functionally important services. It will also inevitably generate frustrations in B and in all probability the corresponding aggressive attitudes and hence will predispose B to a course of action which seeks to retaliate by injuring A, or pursuing his own interests at A's expense. The tendency is to a reciprocal influence, the effect of which is a deepening of conflict, a progressive intensification of antagonisms. The limiting case is the state of affairs which Hobbes has classically formulated as the "war of all against all."

The case of conversion is somewhat different. Its effect may, concretely, be to convert B, who was a deviant personality, to the basic value orientation of the social group, thus mitigating malintegration and potential conflict. But it may also be a case of A, having become attached to a heterodox attitude, converting other members from their orthodoxy to his heterodoxy. The result is, unless as seldom happens, the conversion wins over the whole group, to introduce a division within it which can be the basis of some of the most violent possible conflicts, of which "religious wars" are prominent examples.

When it is a matter of non-rational modes of influence, the situation is at bottom much the same as with the rational. White magic may be an integrating force, as is ritual of the commonly shared positive cult. But above all black magic or "sorcery" may, on occasion, be one of the most dangerous of disintegrating forces. This can be the case in at least two respects. On the one hand, as has been pointed out, A may actually and empirically succeed in injuring B, thus making him fall ill or lose in a fight. The injury is nonetheless real, even though A is ignorant, empirically, of how he was able to inflict it. But, on the other hand, even if the non-rational attempt to influence is actually ineffectual, it can become known that the attempt has been made or is contemplated, and hence can arouse an appropriate affective response in B of hatred or indignation toward A, and be a factor in stimulating him to retaliate in this or other ways.

It is quite clear, then, that no social system could long survive if its members, in trying to influence one another, resorted at random, or as the immediate circumstances indicated to their interests or impulses, to any of the possible means of exerting influence on others which lay at hand. There is a functional necessity for some kind of selective mechanism whereby the modes of influence which are in general favorable to social integration are favored and conversely those tending to disruption of the social system are held in check, if not wholly eliminated. It is, perhaps, legitimate to refer to these as the mechanisms of "social control." Much of the subsequent analysis will be concerned with some of the more important of them.

A somewhat similar problem of integration exists in relation to reciprocal affective attitudes, as such, in abstraction from their accompanying teleological orientations. Before approaching the subject of the mechanisms of social control, it is well to say a few words about these problems.

It is clear that positive personal affects are, generally speaking, favorable to social integration, negative affects are on the whole disruptive. But the balance of these specific affective attitudes toward persons in a social system is very delicate. From the point of view of any given A, it is possible to classify the other actors in the same social system roughly in three categories: those who, as individuals, are positively affectively significant to him – whom, in the broadest sense, he "loves" or with whom he is on friendly terms; those who are negatively significant, to whom he is hostile, or whom he "hates;" and those who are affectively neutral to him. Being an analytical classification, this does not exclude the possibility of ambivalent attitudes toward the same concrete person. Any given B will be in one of these classes, let us say, one of the first two. But the problem of integration arises, not only between A and this B as a reciprocal problem. C is, let us say, affectively positive from A's point of view, but negative from that of B. This fact, if the intensities involved are at all high, cannot fail to have important repercussions on the affective relation of A and B, putting a strain on their friendliness. Hence, not only is it a functional requirement of integration that there should be a control of hostile affects as between pairs of individuals, but that when any two individuals are affectively integrated they should, on the whole, have similar affectual attitudes to all third parties who are affectually important to both of them and who belong in this respect in the same "particular nexus."

Furthermore, one of the most important motives of trying to influence others is to modify their affectual attitudes toward the actor himself or toward third parties. Such an attempt, if successful, naturally calls for a re-equilibration of the whole particular nexus to which both A and B belong. Finally, with regard to claims on the "response" of others, as in so many other respects, legitimate expectations strongly tend to be built up. The effect of shifts in the affectual equilibrium, which are continually occurring in any concrete social system, is to lead to frustrations of these expectations. This, in turn, calls forth, overtly or not, the typical frustration reactions, notably of aggression. One of the most important patterns in this connection is the "jealousy" pattern. Jealousy, in the context of personal affects, is the aggressive reaction toward a person who is felt to be responsible for an attempt to "alienate" from the jealous person, an affective response of security in which he feels he has a legitimate expectation. Jealousy, like most aggressive reactions, may function as a reintegration mechanism insofar as, by putting a stop to the alienation process, it tends to restore the affective equilibrium of the particular nexus. But to be effectively so, it must, in common with other potentially "antisocial" modes of activity, be subject to a rather stringent social control. Nothing can be more disruptive of the stability and effective functioning of a system of social relationships, than if it is honeycombed with intense jealousies. Indeed, their occurrence on a large scale is one of the most significant indices of a serious state of malintegration of the system.

Equally important considerations apply to the implications of the mutuality of moral attitudes for the stability of social systems. Insofar as individuals are the objects of these attitudes they are not simply "respected" or "disapproved." They are "valued." According to the content of the moral codes and the particular circumstances, there is an indefinite number of different possible valuations. Moreover, A never values simply one other individual, B; he evaluates an indefinite number of other individuals, C, D, etc. Value, in this sense, is inherently a quantitative concept, however incapable of measurement. Hence, a valuation of a plurality of different individuals at the same time inherently implies a *relative* valuation, a *ranking* of them, however roughly. The question must always arise whether B or C is the more respected. Even if they are *equally* respected, this is still a quantitative evaluation.

Next, account must be taken of the fact that, as in the case of personal affects, there is a continuous particular nexus involving the mutual evaluations of a plurality of actors. Hence, it is never simply a question of how pairs mutually evaluate each other, while also of how far A's and B's evaluations of C agree. If they agree in their mutual evaluation of each other, but widely disagree about C, but at the same time they both have to associate frequently with him and compare notes about him, strain and potential conflict enter into the situation with disruptive implications. Hence, it is a functional necessity of a stable social system that there should be, at least so far as there is occasion for them to be compared, a relatively stable scale of ranking of the different actors in it.

But such a scale of ranking cannot be agreed upon unless there are, in an adequately corresponding degree, *common standards* according to which the judgments are arrived at, or by which they are determined when called into question. Furthermore, in this, as in the other respect, legitimate expectations as to the evaluation of others, and the corresponding treatment, are built up. Where a person is deprived of what he feels to be the evaluation he deserves, [56] and this is made conspicuous by its being accorded to another, whom A feels deserves the recognition

---

[56] Naturally he himself must be evaluated along with the others.

less than, or no more than he, a reaction of indignation comes into force which is another form of jealousy, this time centering about moral evaluations. One of the most prominent examples is "professional jealousy," which can be just as disruptive as personal affectual jealousy.[57]

There must, then, in any stable social system be a scale of common standards for the relative valuation of individuals. This is its "scale of social stratification." Social stratification in some sense then is one of the most fundamental modes of "structuralization" of the relations of individuals in social systems. But the functional necessity of this scale has a further implication of crucial analytical significance. It can only be a "common" scale, and thus fulfill its functional role, insofar as it constitutes the application, in the relevant connection, of a common moral code or value-orientation. This "common value system" has a functional significance not only in this, but in a variety of other contexts as well.

Questions of social stratification have to do with "integral" valuations of the individual as a whole, which may, in turn, be a function of various elements, such as, the valuation of specific qualities and achievements, wealth, birth, authority, etc. But when the problem of the stability of social systems is approached from the point of view of modes of mutual influence of individuals, the unit of reference is the type of action rather than the actor as a total unit. It has already been seen that recourse to such modes of influence as fraud, coercion, compulsion, propaganda, black magic, and, in certain circumstances, conversion may, if uncontrolled, have dangerously disruptive consequences. The question arises of how this functionally necessary control is brought about.

In terms of the scheme of analysis followed throughout this essay, a controlling factor may be located either "externally" to the actor as a part of the situation, as an obstacle or an inducement to carry out a given line of action; or it may be "subjective," a matter of his orientation to the situation. It was Hobbes who most thoroughly explored the possibilities of accounting for the repression of force and fraud by external factors,

---

[57] On the jealousy pattern generally, see Kingsley Davis, "Jealousy and Sexual Property," *Social Forces*, 14: 395-405 (March, 1936).

notably the threat of coercive sanctions. The great difficulty of this solution lies in its generalization from the case of the individual actor to the social system as a whole, for there must be someone to apply the sanctions and the question then arises of where the guarantee is that this agency will apply them in the interests of the collectivity as a whole rather than in their own interests at the expense of others and with disruptive rather than integrative consequences. Hobbes tried to solve this problem by his theory of the social contract and the role of the sovereign, but much of his reasoning is forced and far-fetched.

The tendency of more recent analytical thinking is to throw much stronger emphasis on the subjective possibility and to relegate coercive sanctions to a secondary, although by no means unimportant, role.[58] This line of analysis involves the theorem that, in some sense, the solution of the problem lies in the fact that there exist mechanisms whereby the average member of a social system is conditioned not to *want* to secure his own advantage at the expense of others, at least to a socially dangerous extent. This implies that the different actors' teleological and affectual orientations are integrated to the extent that they do not lead to an intolerable amount of disruptive conflict. This would seem to imply, as has already been pointed out, a predominance of friendly over hostile personal affective attitudes toward these various types of action. And these moral attitudes must involve some common "agreement" on principles, as to the moral quality of different types of action and, at least among the potentially disruptive types, as to the circumstances in which their use is justified. This "agreement" need not be to any considerable extent a matter of explicit intellectual formulation; an agreement of practical moral attitude in the relevant situations is sufficient. But some minimum of practical agreement as to the "rights" of other members of the collectivity is essential. This is, in fact, an aspect of *common* value-orientation, an integration on the level of moral sentiments.

[58] Which includes their symbolic role in relation to sentiments. See, especially, Durkheim's theory of punishment [in the analysis of mechanical solidarity in Emile Durkheim, *The Division of Labor in Society* (New York: Macmillan, 1933), Book One, Chapter Two – V.L.].

The existence of these moral sentiments is manifested by typical reactions of individuals in case of the contravention of the corresponding norms – in the case of contravention by others in the form of moral indignation, if on the part of the actor himself, feelings of guilt, shame, and remorse. The widespread occurrence of these reactions, and the circumstances in which they occur, give ample empirical evidence supporting this general analysis. A notable recent addition to this evidence has been the discovery, by psychoanalytic methods, of the extremely important role in the neurotic personality of *repressed* guilt feelings caused by the violation or desire to violate norms which, on the conscious level, the individual may not at all be aware of being morally obligated to.

Thus by another analytical path than that of following out the implications of the functional necessity of relative valuation of individuals, the role of the common system of moral norms has been arrived at. It goes without saying that, in the integrated case, the system must, in the two contexts, be the same system, and for a social collectivity to function at all, there must be a relatively high degree of integration between them, for otherwise seriously disruptive conflict would result.

Thus it may be concluded that "social control" requires above all two things: a relative predominance of favorable or "solidary" personal affects over hostile ones, and of moral respect for other individuals in the same social system over disapproval; and, secondly, the common orientation of the actors in the social system for common choices of ends, particularly ultimate ends, and of means, particularly in the field of influencing the action of others, as well as making a consistent and common scale of relative evaluation of the different individuals possible.[59]

---

[59] In the literature of social and psychological theory, there has been a great deal of controversy between "rationalist" and "anti-intellectualist" schools of thought. Most of this controversy has taken place on a plane which is largely irrelevant to the present analysis and it does not seem necessary to take a critical attitude to it. In view of the prominence of the controversy, however, it is well to state more explicitly just what the role of the cognitive element in personality integration is conceived to be.

It is not a question of action being in any simple sense "determined" by ideas, nor is it a question of its being determined by other factors. The cognitive mode of orientation is, so far as action is described and analyzed in terms of the present frame of reference, only one of the basic modes of orientation, but nonetheless an essential one.

Cognitive orientation is, like any other aspect of action, subject to normative standards, the norms of "rationality." As in all such cases, the actual state of affairs falls far short of complete conformity with these normative standards. Not only the theoretical possibility, but the actual facts of ignorance and error are of crucial empirical importance to systems of action. But again, as in all such cases, the fact of lack of full conformity is not to be taken to mean that the normative standard is unimportant, but only that it is one among several factors determining the action. Lack of conformity does not imply that, if the normative standard did not exist, the action would not be radically different.

One of the principal aspects of the normative standard in this case is "cognitive integration." Of this there are two principal criteria, clarity and consistency. The first implies the greatest possible definiteness and precision of concepts and statements, the second their logical integration into mutually consistent systems. Full cognitive integration of a personality would imply that the actor had clear and precise ideas about each aspect of his situation and of the normative patterns to which his action was subject, and that in each context the ideas thus held were logically consistent with those held in other contexts. There can be little doubt of the presence of the tendency to cognitive integration or of its very great importance in action.

It must not, however, be forgotten that cognitive integration is only one aspect of the more general tendency to integration of personality. Each important cognitive element is to a greater or lesser degree integrated with non-cognitive elements, both teleological and affective. Precisely because, in other respects as well as the cognitive, the normal actor is imperfectly integrated, and because in many contexts the other elements are dominant over the cognitive, it is not surprising that there are teleological and affective elements often underlying ignorance and error, as in the phenomenon of "wishful thinking." The optimum condition of cognitive development and integration is one involving a specific combination of the other, non-cognitive factors, and such a combination is, in actual situations, not often present.

One further point should be explicitly mentioned. The *role* of cognitive elements in the determination of action cannot be judged solely in terms of the self-consciousness of the ordinary individual actor on the cognitive level. It is necessary rather to study the question on a comparative basis and over long periods for large masses of people. Very generally the "ideas" which are most important to the action of a group are implicit in their practical attitudes rather than explicitly self-conscious. In a sense, they become part of the uncritically accepted "definition of the situation" rather than of the "wishes" of the individual actors. See the author's paper, "The Role of Ideas in Social Action," *op. cit.*

V. The Integration of Personality and the Relation of Individual Motivation to the Stability of Social Systems

"Action" is always a matter of the behavior of individuals, never of collectivities as a "unit." What is usually referred to as the unitary behavior of collectivities is the complex result of the different actions of all the component actors. This remains true, for analytical purposes, no matter how highly integrated or "well coordinated" these actions may be.

The analysis of the conditions and mechanisms maintaining the stability of social systems, then, leads directly to that of the motivation of their component individual actors. The actor, as well as the social system, is a "going concern." As such, as a sub-system of the social system of action, he is subject to certain functional necessities which can be given in turn the same sort of analysis which has just been applied to the larger social system. These functional necessities submit him to the necessity of "orientation" to two main orders of "conditions" without which he could not continue to function. One is the system of conditions of "survival" as a unit analytically isolated from social relationships. The other is the set of conditions imposed by the fact that he participates in such a set of relationships and he either plays a functionally significant role in the "economy" of the social system as a whole, or it is a functional necessity of the collectivity that he should be prevented from going too far in the direction of playing potentially disruptive roles.

It hardly needs to be pointed out that the actor, as a "going concern," is characterized by a mode of "integration" which is logically similar to that of the social system. The various elements of his "personality," which have been analytically distinguished, need to work in "harmony" without causing conflict and the resulting tensions, or at least without seriously interfering with each other. The development of the theory of psychopathology in the last generation has brought impressive evidence in favor of the importance of integration of personality in this sense. For all schools seem to be substantially agreed on the fundamental importance of conflict as a factor in abnormal behavior and states. Indeed, the existence of "unsolved" conflicts beyond a certain level of emotional intensity, and of importance for the individual, might well serve as one of the most important criteria of the "pathological" personality.

Personal integration then requires a significant degree of coordination between the different modes of orientation, so that the tendencies of action arising from any one fit "appropriately" with those of the others. In considering this, in its bearing on the problem of motivation, it is important to realize that any given actor must be thought of as oriented in all three of the principal modes at the same time, and, within each category of orientation, in each of the important subsidiary respects. He is thus oriented at the same time to a set of normative patterns and an existent situation. His cognitive orientation to the existing situation contains both empirical and non-empirical elements which must to some degree be mutually consistent. Thus, he cannot hold a non-empirical theory, so far as he is integrated on the cognitive level, which is flatly in contradiction with his empirical knowledge. If such contradictions exist, they are potential points of strain about which may center specific re-integrative mechanisms. Further his non-empirical cognitive orientation must be such as to make his normative patterns meaningful, while the normative patterns in turn must be such as are, in some significant degree, capable of realization in the empirical situation as he knows it. Furthermore, his non-empirical cognitive picture must generally in some significant degree supply a plausible explanation of the more basic impossibilities and frustrations in the realization of the relevant wishes and normative patterns.

The normative patterns will, in part, define the goals and ends of his teleological orientation, and the "normative conditions" under which they may or should be pursued, the rules, particularly with regard to respecting the "rights" of others, to which his action is subject. Moreover, they supply the content of the moral standards by which the rightness and desirability of the action of others and of the actor himself are judged, and which also define certain of his attitudes to the non-human situation and to objects in it. Here non-empirical cognitive orientation is primarily significant in giving meaning to teleological orientations; empirical in facilitating the practical carrying out of teleological trends and in saving wasted effort by making the actor aware of obstacles and impossibilities. In the context of actual or potential frustrations, it helps in turn to define the situation in which the non-empirical explanation of the meaning of such frustrations is sought.

Finally, all three modes of affective orientation must be to a significant degree integrated with this whole structure. Pleasurable feelings must be aroused by things and situations which are on the whole consistent with the recognized normative patterns. Impulses to attain pleasure must not, at the cost of excessive frustration, be continually running against blank impossibilities. The actor must know how to minimize his exposure to painful situations. Then the attachment to objects and persons must, to a degree, be such as is permissible within the relevant normative patterns, meaningful within his non-empirical cognitive orientation, and reasonably capable of actual realization and not in general too painful. Conversely his negative affects, his hatreds and dislikes must be integrated with these other elements. Finally, the other two affectual modes need to be integrated with the system of moral sentiments. The latter is primarily a name for the actor's affectual orientation to at least one fundamental aspect of the system of normative patterns to which he is subject. But there may be conflicts in loving what one disapproves, in feeling guilty pleasure in actions which are morally taboo, etc.

The individual personality is, from this point of view, in a delicate state of equilibrium of all these different modes of orientation, an equilibrium which, unless he is an extreme "pathological case," involves a relative degree of integration with each other. How is this equilibrated system articulated to the broader social system of which it is a part?

The primary functional requirement of the social system in this context is clear; it is, negatively, that the integration of the individual personality should not take a direction which would lead it on a large scale into activities disruptive of the stability of the social system, positively that, so far as possible, it should have teleological tendencies directly conducive to the promotion of its functionally important patterns of action. The accomplishment of this necessary coordination by wholly "external" pressures not only raises very difficult problems of visualizing the necessary social organization; it seems highly improbable in view of the importance, in the individual personality, of integration. If the dominant teleological tendencies of the great bulk of the individuals in a social system were, in fact, anything like random relative to the normative patterns enforced by the "sovereign," this process of enforcement would entail an amount of frustration on a grand scale which there is every reason to believe could not be supported. There would be so much explosive material accumulated in the social system that it is not conceivable that there could be a sovereign authority strong enough to maintain stability by such coercive methods.

The focal point of articulation is a set of *common* normative patterns. These can be of a wide variety of different types, but for present purposes the most crucially important are those which carry moral authority. Social integration with respect to these implies primarily two, reciprocally related, things. First, the moral norms with which the various individuals are integrated as persons constitute a common system. This does not imply that all the moral standards are the same in all respects, for the individuals may be differentiated as to social role. But it does imply that where their actionsystems come into contact, there is integration. This must mean that, in some sense, the particular standards are all subsumed, or capable of being subsumed, under the same set of general "principles." Very often the principles are either wholly implicit or, at most, clearly explicit only in the minds of a very small, particularly self-conscious, minority.

The second, reciprocal, aspect of this integration is that the individual personalities are, on the whole, integrated with the common moral patterns. This is what is decisive for the problem of motivation. It is not enough that the average individual should merely "assent" to the moral authority of a norm. Most murderers would readily assent to the first commandment. They, and the appropriate moral sentiments, must be built into the structure of an integrated personality in the sense in which this is the counterfoil of the conception of a "pathological case."

Though most of the materials necessary for doing it have already been introduced into the discussion, the carrying through of the analysis of just how this works out would lead much too far afield. Brief mention may, however, be made of one very important aspect of the problem. Much of the historical discussion of the problem of "social control" has been couched in terms of the problem of "egoism" or "self-interest" vs. "altruism." On account of certain features of the tradition of Western thought,[60] there has been a strong tendency to treat this dichotomy as one of typical concrete motives of particular acts or chains of action. Precisely the classical Hobbesian version of the "problem of order" was put in terms of the difficulty of controlling men's "egoistic" tendencies of behavior or, as he called them, "passions." Even moral norms have often tended to be thought of, as by Kant, as something "coercing" the actor into conformity with a pattern against the opposition of his "natural" inclinations.

The view to which the present analysis leads up is very different from this. It is that "human nature" is a very plastic entity with no specific "motives" or even tendencies of behavior. In the long process of social "conditioning" from birth on, it is gradually molded into the concrete personality-structure of the adult, which may be exceedingly different according to the nature of the conditioning influences to which it has been exposed. Whatever direction the development takes, the main tendency is to the development of relatively integrated personalities, integrated internally as a system and integrated with the requirements and patterns of the larger social system. In the reciprocal interaction of individual and social systems, the individual will develop relatively stable directions of teleological orientation, integrated with the appropriate cognitive systems and affects. He will, to a very large extent, share his

60 See *The Structure of Social Action*, *op. cit.*, especially Chapter III.

cognitive orientation and normative patterns with the other actors in the same social system. The others will, at the same time, develop "expectations" as to what is, for any given individual in any given situation, proper or "reasonable" conduct.

On *both* sides of the reciprocal relationship, there tends to be an integration of *all* the principal motivation elements. The normal individual tends on the whole to "want" what is in conformity with the normative, especially moral, patterns which are built into his own personality, to experience "satisfaction" in achieving the relevant ends, in possessing the relevant qualities, etc. His motivation in any given case is made up of both self-interested and disinterested elements. But the same is true, broadly, of the other individuals in the same social system. Hence they will tend to approve conduct in conformity with their own normative patterns and to disapprove conduct in violation of them.

This fact makes it possible for the "disinterested" elements in the motivation of any one individual to be strongly reinforced, in their effectiveness in controlling his conduct, by the impingement on him of the consequences of the fact that others also have such disinterested elements in their own motivation. For, from the point of view of a given individual, among the most important sources of "satisfaction" of what can justifiably be called the self-interested elements of his own motivation, are things dependent on the "good will" of others, notably their willingness to assist, or at least not obstruct, him in the attainment of pleasure, their affective response to him, and the recognition they can accord him. When his conduct is such as to influence them not to grant him these sources of satisfaction, it may go still farther and entail positive dissatisfaction. The other may inflict pain, he may not only withdraw positive response but actively hate the first actor, or he may go beyond refusing recognition and actively run down the other's reputation. In all these cases, the fact that such sentiments are normally integrated with teleological tendencies is of the greatest importance. For not only does an individual have affective attitudes toward another, he tends to take action appropriate to these attitudes, he tends, as Pareto put it, "to manifest his sentiments by external acts." Positive affectual attitudes are normally accompanied by acts favorable to the interests of their object, negative affects by acts detrimental to those interests.

The effect of all these things on the actor toward whom they are directed does not work out only through the mechanisms of rational "taking account," but also in various non-logical ways. But, generally speaking, it can be said that any serious tendency for action to take a course conspicuously deviant from the accepted normative patterns sets in motion a whole range of forces adversely impinging on the self-interest of the deviant actor, forces which tend to restore the equilibrium by giving him entirely adequate motivation to conformity with what is, on the one hand, his own "conscience" but, on the other hand, at the same time, the expectation of others to whom he looks for help, pleasure, response, and recognition.

It should hardly need to be pointed out that the above discussion is primarily concerned with the "ideal type" of both an integrated human personality and an integrated social system. There is no implication whatever that actual personalities and social systems conform closely to this type. Obviously they do so only in widely varying degrees and never by any means fully. There is, however, a sense in which they "tend" to conform to it. It is exactly the sense in which an organism "tends" to conform to a state of "health" and to throw off or recuperate from "disease." In biology and medicine, it is quite possible to use the concepts of health and disease without anyone assuming that the author is guilty of thinking that all organisms are perfectly healthy and there is no such thing as disease. The difficulties, on a general methodological level, of the concept of "integration" as applied to social systems and to personalities, are neither more nor less formidable than those attached to the concept of health in biology and medicine. Indeed, it is, in both cases, the logically necessary point of reference for any analysis of the modes and mechanisms of "malintegration" or of "pathological" states and behavior. But there is no intention whatever of trying to minimize the empirical importance of these pathological phenomena. [61]

[61] It is extremely important to place the study of malintegration, hence, of pathological phenomena, in the context of a clearly conceived conception of an integrated system on both the personal and the social levels. Failure to do this adequately has led to an important "pathological bias" in generalized theory, notably among the psychoanalysts. One of the most notable examples is Freud's *Totem and Taboo* (London: Routledge, 1919). What is done is essentially to take the elements and personality structures found in neurotic individuals and generalize on them without regard to the danger of involvement in the fallacy of misplaced concreteness. A recent example from the pen of a sociologist which, however, is much milder than some of the more extravagant psychoanalytic theories, is to be found in Willard Waller, *The Family; A Dynamic Interpretation* (New York: The Cordon Company, 1938). Professor Waller is involved in this bias in his interpretation of the role of romanticism and his view of the *inherent* instability of the marriage relationship.

This is not, of course, to say that psychoanalytic theory is in general unimportant or erroneous in its relations to the theory of action. On the contrary, it is of crucial importance at many points, a few of which have been barely indicated in the course of the discussion. But its fruitfulness for the theory of action depends on its successful integration with those aspects of the latter which are altogether outside of the range of psychoanalytic interest or competence, such as, economic theory or the analysis of transcendental religious orientation. This integration requires a great deal of critical interpretation of the psychoanalytic literature. Fortunately, there are signs that internal developments from the psychoanalytic side are doing much to narrow the gap. Notable examples are the two recent books of Karen Horney, *The Neurotic Personality of Our Time* (New York: Norton, 1937) and *New Ways in Psychoanalysis* (*op. cit.*).

VI. Modes of Structuralization of Social Systems

A. The Generalized Framework of Social Structure: Status

The present analysis started with some of the most "elementary" structural elements of social action, and their relations. By analyzing these structural elements and relations and calling attention to various of their possible modes of combination, it has gradually and laboriously come a little closer to the concrete level of what we mean by "social" action and structure on the level of the "common sense" of the social sciences. But so far the tendency has been to deal only with the various elements of the individual concrete "act," with the human individual as a system of action, and with social systems only insofar as they involve the mere fact of a plurality of acting individuals. It is now possible to take a decisive further step, and introduce considerations of the functional differentiation of large-scale, interindividual systems of action, and of the differentiation of individuals as "social types" within the same social system.

There are three different levels on which it will be necessary to consider these modes of "structuralization" of action in social systems. By this term is meant the development of certain relative "uniformities" and "rigidities" in the system which lend it a definite "form," making it more than an "amorphous" or "unorganized" plurality, on the one hand, of actions and, on the other hand, of personalities. The first of these is a matter of certain modes of structuralization of the phenomenon of *order* or integration in relating individuals to one another independently of the specific functional content of the individuals, actions, or their types. The second is a matter of modes in which the specific acts and sub-systems of action of the individuals become differentiated in ways coordinated with that of other individuals. And, third, there is differentiation of individual types themselves.

Integration, it has been shown, involves the orientation of action to an order, to normative patterns conformity with which is recognized as an obligation of the actor. There seem to be three principal modes in which, in general terms, this order tends to structuralize the relations of individual actors.

In the first place, it has been shown that it is impossible for the actors of a social system to have strong moral sentiments without each subjecting the others to relative evaluation, while being himself in turn subject to ranking, according to a more or less definite scale. One primary aspect of the order to which the actors in the system are oriented is, then, the scale of stratification. It is functionally impossible for there to be a social system made up of the elements treated in this analysis without its component individuals being "ordered" to some degree in terms of stratification.

Second, the fact of potential mutual influence is of crucial functional importance. Certain possible modes are potentially dangerous to the stability of the social system. Hence there must be some mode of orientation to an order which defines different attitudes toward these modes on different occasions – which of them are permissible, which mandatory, which prohibited. There seem to be two sub-aspects of this regulation of mutual influence. There is, first, the phenomenon of authority. Sometimes it is functionally necessary to the social system for some individuals to be in a position to influence the attitudes and actions of others regardless of whether the latter wish it or consent to being so influenced. Such a position, so far as it is legitimized in terms of a common normative order, is a position of "authority." Secondly, conversely, it is sometimes necessary for individuals, who might be subject to modes of influence which are subjectively undesirable to them, or undesirable to the society, to be protected from them. The prohibition of affecting the individual through such undesirable modes of influence on the part of others, in terms of the common order, may be called the protection of "rights."

The existence of authority which is morally legitimized in terms of a common value system, and of rights which are "protected" in the same terms, is thus a functional necessity of any social system. The actual content and distribution of authority, on the other hand, are matters of the specific value system, the specific modes of differentiation of the social structure in the other respects, and, finally, of the particular situational circumstances in which it is located.

The third fundamental "structuralization" of social systems on this level is what may be called the "definition of roles." In one main aspect, this is a consequence of a fundamental phenomenon to which attention has been called several times, namely, the fact that, from the point of view of any given actor, there are "expectations" relative to the behavior of others. Conversely, others build up expectations as to the actor's own behavior. A second basis of the phenomenon lies in the fact that stability of the system of action of the individual demands that it be structured, that it be not a random collection of all the different possible, and functionally important, modes of action, but that these possibilities should be segregated and arranged in a manner that is appropriate to the shifting situations in which the actor is placed, notably, although not exclusively, as given in terms of "what the others are doing," and compatible with the individual's need for personal integration. Thus, the different "responses" either will not interfere with one another or will positively contribute to the life process as a whole. This means that there should be stable differentiations into separate types of actions. These, in the nature of the case, become bound up with expectations and with the actors' own feelings of self-esteem. Finally, they, like the order defining authority and rights, become integrated with the common value system. Insofar, then, as in a relatively stable manner a certain relatively specific mode of behavior is expected, and that expectation is sanctioned in terms of the common value system, the actor will be said to be performing a "role" and, correspondingly, to occupy a "status."

The term status is, however, broader than this. Its main reference is to the "location" of an individual actor in the "social structure." In a functionally relevant sense, that is, as a "normal" member of the group, an actor's status will always be defined, on the most general level, in terms of the three "modalities" of status which have just been discussed, in terms of his place in the scale of stratification and its various component valuations, in terms of his relation to the structure of authority and rights, and in terms of his place with reference to defined roles. Such a "position" will only be called a "status" insofar as it is sanctioned in terms of a common value-orientation, that is, as it is "institutionalized." It is clear that the positions which are most important in defining the actor to himself and to others as a "social personality," and which define the "legitimate" expectations of others in relation to him, are always institutionalized in this sense, in proportion as the system as a whole is integrated. For an integrated system of action always includes a system of moral norms.

B. Functional Differentiation of the Action System of the Individual

It has been seen that the individual actor cannot "act" at random, shifting from one possible mode of action to another without organization. In the first place, the organization of his action system must be functionally adapted to the exigencies of the situation. Secondly, it must be adapted to the necessities of a relatively smoothly functioning "integration," so that strains and conflicts are minimized. There are many different aspects of this differentiation of the action-system of an individual. Only certain of the crudest can be gone into here.

There is, logically inherent in the structure of action, one basic criterion of differentiation. On the one hand, action may be functionally significant because of its relatively direct relation, in the role of means, to the attainment of important goals or ends. Insofar as this aspect is dominant, it may be called "goal-directed" activity. On the other hand, it may consist in activities which, from this point of view, are relatively "functionless" or "useless," which, in the broadest terms, the actor performs as "ends in themselves." This class of activities may be called the "expressional" system of action.

One or two things need to be said about the general status of the distinction. Like all classifications of concrete phenomena, it is relative in empirical application, with a gradual transition between the types according to the relevant criteria. An example of this relativity is the use of the term "direct" in defining goal-directed activity. It would be clearly out of the question to imply that expressional activities had no "function" in the equilibrium of the system, that it would "make no difference" if they were suppressed *in toto*. Quite the contrary is the case. But the "functions" of expressional activities in relation to goals are generally "latent" rather than "manifest,"[62] they are indirect through mechanisms which require a technical analysis to understand. They are not functionally related to goals for immediately *descriptive* purposes. Secondly, as should be clear but has not been emphasized in this essay, concrete action occurs in complex systems with immediate goals and varying orders of remoter goals until the ultimate goals are reached. What is, concretely, classed as expressional activity, may, while the total course of action is best classed as expressional, involve immediate goals the process of attainment of which is clearly goal-directed. This concrete criss-crossing of the classification is of peculiar significance to the structure of social systems, since many goals which are on a broader basis primarily of an expressional significance become the object of relatively permanent specialized roles, and become perhaps the dominant goals of the goal-directed activities of the performers of these roles. The classification must, then, be made in two different contexts, on the one hand, from the point of view of the functional significance of the activity in the *total* system of action being considered, on the other hand, from that of the *immediate* context of the specific individual acts. What is, in the former context, expressional may well be, in the latter, very largely goal-directed.

Finally, there is one further general caution. Most classifications, such as the above, may be used in different methodological contexts. On

---

62 A distinction used, though not yet in published form, by Professor Robert K. Merton.

the one hand, it may be used to define types, and to discriminate concrete cases which come more or less close to each of the types thus defined. In such a context, there are always borderline cases which are transitional between the types. On the other hand, it may be used on a more analytical level to discriminate elements, of one kind or another, which combine to form the concrete cases. In that case, a concrete instance does not "belong" to an element, or "approximate" it, but is "made up" in different ways, and in varying proportions, of the different elements. The classification being discussed at present is subject to analysis and application in both ways. Above all from the "broader" point of view, it is used to discriminate the general classes of activity into which the action system of a given actor is differentiated. But, at the same time, when a closer analysis of particular acts or courses of action is needed, it is usually possible to identify *both* goal-directed and expressional elements in the same concrete act. Then the differentiation of types, and approximation to them on the broader level, becomes a matter of variations in the proportions and mode of combination of the elements.

Both goal-directed and expressional activities are subject to subclassification. Such classification involves many different criteria, and the more detailed it is, the more complex it becomes. It is impossible, here, to attempt anything more than the crudest outline of a few of the most important criteria and types.

It is clear that the concept of goal-direction implies a mode of orientation to the situation, because the attainment of a goal is an alteration in the potential relation of the actor to his situation. The most fundamental distinction which has had to be made in the present essay touching the situation is that between the empirical and non-empirical aspects of the situation. Furthermore, this distinction impinges on goal-directed activity in two different ways. On the one hand, the distinction may apply to the goals toward which action is oriented, which may refer to empirical states of affairs or to "transcendental" states. On the other hand, in seeking the attainment of either type, the actor may be oriented to conditions and means which are empirical, or to his conception of the relevance in the role of means and conditions of non-empirical agencies and entities.

The primary distinction seems to be that of types of ends or goals. Teleological orientation to empirical ends is the central focus of one of the basic systems of activity; orientation to transcendental ends or, more broadly, teleological adjustment of the actor to the non-empirical situation is the focus of another system.

Each of these is subject to various sub-classifications. No attempt will be made to be exhaustive under either heading, but only to call attention to certain basic types. In the empirical context, there are two that seem to be of primary importance. One, which a Western mind immediately thinks of, is the system of "rational expediencies" – the system of action where the rational means-end relationship forms the dominant *normative* standard, regardless of how closely it is in fact adhered to, and of how far non-logical mechanisms, such as, habituation, play a part in the determination of action. This, in turn, subdivides into two main subsystems: "technology," the choice of means according to the norm of efficiency, for specific ends; and "economizing," the allocation of scarce means between alternative ends in terms of the norm of "economy." The two may join together in being oriented to "expediency." Other individuals, in this context, come in only as means and conditions of the attainment of the ends of the first actor.

The other most important modes of teleological orientation to empirical goals are those which involve non-logical normative standards. The ritual types seem to be the most important, where the decisive criteria are symbolic appropriateness and the element of respect for the sacred. In relation to empirical ends, ritual systems can be, following anthropological usage, spoken of as "magic." Magic is functionally associated with the limitations on adequacy of rational empirical knowledge and control. Where conditions are unfavorable to the development of ritual, either because the culture tends to exclude sacredness from a secular sphere or because there is a general attitude hostile to traditionalism, it is by no means out of the question that these gaps should be filled by other, functionally equivalent, mechanisms. How far, however, these involve orientation, not only to goals, but to normative standards of the selection of procedures which are neither empirically rational nor ritual, is a question.

Teleological orientation in goal-directed activity, to non-empirical aspects of the situation that have the sacred quality of the "supernatural order" will be called "religious" action. Religious action seems to have two primary forms. Though goal-directed, its goals will, in general, not be empirical states of affairs, but transcendental. It is, hence, out of the question that they should be pursued by empirically rational techniques. But there is a most important type which assimilates as closely as possible to this. That is, it becomes a matter, so far as possible, of the rational application of a *theory* of non-empirical reality and its relation to man. On the basis of this theory, then, action is directed to the attainment of such supernatural ends as "salvation" and "Nirvana" by the application of specific means which, in terms of the theory, are adapted to the end. This is particularly common in cases of the practice of mystical and contemplative techniques and certain forms of asceticism.

The other principal mode of religious action seems to be the ritual. The only essential difference between religious and magical ritual is that the former is not oriented to empirical goals. Hence, functionally, it is not associated with what are in the same sense the "inadequacies" of knowledge and control, but with human interests and affects beyond what are, in the culture in question, the recognized limits of such knowledge and control. Wherever there is an established feeling that a thing *cannot* be known or controlled by empirical techniques, or *cannot* be understood empirically, but at the same time that aspect of the situation cannot be left aside as indifferent without strain and frustration, there is apt to be religious ritual. The type case is death, which cannot be a matter of indifference in human groups. But the acceptance of death as an inevitable fact is so deep-rooted, that there is, in general, no thought of abolishing it or of bringing the dead back to life. The direct goals of funeral ritual are always transcendental. Its effects on empirical social action are indirect, through functional mechanisms. Religious ritual, like magical, is subject to elaborate sub-classification which cannot be gone into here.

Again the possibility should not be excluded that there are other *normatively* significant modes of teleological orientation to the supernatural order, just as there may be important modes of orientation to aspects of the non-empirical situation other than the supernatural. These, whatever they may be, have not emerged or become important in the work of the writer of the present essay.

It is understood throughout this discussion that any one of the subsystems of action under analysis is part of a relatively integrated total system of action. This implies that the relation of the specific content of any one such system to that of the others is a matter of great importance. Before turning to the analysis of the expressional systems, a few words may be said about some of the more important of the relations of the empirical-teleological and the religious systems.

One way of getting at the analysis of the functional significance of religion, including ideas of the supernatural order as well as "religious action," is to show some of the functional difficulties which would be encountered by an exclusively empirical-teleological orientation of action. Given the content of typical goals, there are inherent inadequacies of knowledge and control which, given also what is essential to energetic pursuit of goals, namely, that there is strong affective involvement in them, inevitably lead to frustration on a considerable scale. It has already been remarked that magic is a most important functional mechanism in "covering" these gaps. Furthermore, there are, as in the case of death, certain basic frustrations where, in the ordinary technological sense, it is meaningless to try to "do" anything about the situation. Also there is the whole problem of the choice of goals, to which empirical knowledge is inadequate.

Ordinarily the "function" of a religious orientation to the supernatural order is to give "meaning" to frustrations of various sorts and, positively, also to give meaning to the devotion of energy to the currently accepted empirical goals and normative patterns. It, furthermore, is connected with a variety of mechanisms, particularly ritual, which have the related function of reducing the tensions involved in frustrations and conflicts, both within the individual actor and between individuals.

But the very fact that religious orientation is non-empirical, to an "order" which transcends the empirical, means that there is the possibility, not only that this orientation may "sanction" the empirical order and accepted normative patterns, but that there may develop transcendental goals of action. It may even be said that a certain modicum of this *teleological* orientation to the supernatural order is inherent in the existence of ritual, which is omnipresent, particularly in primitive societies. When that happens there is a problem, however latent, of the relative value of this class of goals and of various classes on the empirical level. The "normal" situation, one may say, is for them to be relatively well integrated, though naturally there are all sorts of possibilities as to relative priority. [63] But particularly in view of the numerous possibilities of malintegration, frustration, and affective strain in social systems, varying types and degrees of conflict may arise. Indeed, the very ubiquity of religion is testimony to the fact that social systems, in general, however important the "tendency" to integration, are not stably integrated in relation to constant conditions in a sense which would imply the negligible importance of such strains. The effect of certain of these strains may be to lead to a re-orientation in the course of which some transcendental

[63] Integration here does not necessarily mean "reduction" of either to terms of the other. Transcendental orientations can, so far as they become dominant, lead to the complete devaluation of worldly ends *and* activities. Then the actor becomes indifferent to worldly things or actively combats their temptations, as in asceticism. Calvinism, however, is a notable case of a type of orientation which places a powerful sanction on active participation in worldly occupations, though to be sure not only on those, and the modes of conducting them, which are sanctioned in terms of the basically transcendental ends.
Hedonism, on the other hand, is the mode of integration antithetical to all of these. Its non-empirical orientation, which is often not acknowledged to be such, is employed to sanction the pursuit of worldly ends for their own sake. Most types are intermediate between these extremes.

goals are brought into a place of great prominence and their conflict with certain empirical goals becomes acute.[64] Such a re-orientation will, of course, have a cognitive aspect, but by no means be confined to that.

So long as it is a matter of specific goals or classes of goals on the empirical level, the affect of reorientation with reference to transcendental considerations may be simply to shift the system of "control" of empirical wishes and their satisfactions. But pushed to the extreme, it can become a devaluation of *all* empirical goals or the direct mandate of supernatural sources of authority. When this point is reached, a new order of "need" arises, the need for "salvation." It is this which is one of the most prominent characteristics of the anti-traditional prophetic religious movements. The pursuit of salvation cannot be carried on without articulation with the empirical world and without relations of direct sanction, toleration, or direct disapproval of the many different types of empirical goals. This interweaving, on both the levels of the "sanctioning" of given empirical goal-systems and that of its subordination to a search for "salvation," of the empirical and transcendental orientations to goals, is of crucial empirical importance in social systems of action.

"Expressional" systems of action are those which, as systems, are not oriented to the achievement of specific goals. It is certain that they have important "functions" in the equilibrium of the system of action of the individual, hence of the social system, but these functions are "latent." On the "manifest" level, they are activities which are performed "for their own sake." In general terms any activity that can be engaged in with this attitude can form part of the expressional system. No more than in the case of the goal-directed systems can any classification be exhaustive. This is, indeed, one of the more obscure portions of the theory of action and there is very little systematic analysis in the literature to go on. A differentiation of four important classes may, however, be hazarded.

---

[64] See particularly Max Weber, *Gesammelte Aufsätze zur Religionssoziologie*, *op. cit.*, volume I.

In the first place, there is the type of activity which is most nearly performed purely because people "like to do it," which may be called "play." [65] The system of activity as such not only has no manifest goals, but it is bound by no specific norms which are primary to itself. The only consideration, besides whether the actor "wishes" to do it sufficiently to devote the requisite energy to it, is that of efficiency and economy on attaining the immediate subsidiary goals. Thus, if a man "enjoys" mountain climbing, there may be rather complicated technical problems to solve touching routes, procedures, equipment, etc. Naturally, like all activity, play is bound by norms which keep it from interfering unduly with other people and with other action systems of the same individual. But this is true of all the structuralizations of action. [66]

The second type of expressional activity is that in which there is a definite primary normative orientation to the creation of, or conformity with, certain "forms" which are valued for their own sake. This is perhaps aptly called "art." However the normative standards of art may be defined, as "beauty" or what not, in artistic creation it *matters* what one does, and what results from it, in a sense in which that is not true of play. Whatever the elements of relativity in artistic standards, there can be no doubt of the fact that artistic work is subject to such standards and measured by them.

---

65 This definition does not imply that such activity is, analytically considered, motivated "hedonistically" or in terms of "self-interest." The concept "expressional" activity implies that what is expressed is in general, though in varying combinations in different contexts, *all* the elements of personality structure. It is true that such activity is usually free from "external" pressures – to participate is not generally a "duty." But it has already been pointed out that conformity with normative patterns in many cases constitutes a source of "satisfaction."

66 It is equally true of all modes of structuralization that they generally involve "secondary" relations to other modes of structuralization. This is above all true in that symbolic interrelations grow up and, in conformity with the principle of symbolic appropriateness, there tends to be a certain "congruence" of pattern running through the different fields. Thus, play activities are, very generally, closely bound up with social stratification and symbolically related to it. Certain forms of play enjoy high social status, while the reverse is true of others. It is also possible for authority exercised in a play relationship to be symbolically related to authority in other spheres.

The third type is that in which the orientation is not to impersonal standards, but to a person as such. It has already been pointed out how important persons are as foci of affective attitudes. It is natural, then, that there should be systems of activity focusing on the manifestation of these attitudes in symbolically appropriate form. There seems to be no one suitable term of this class, but activities described by such terms as the expression of "love," "friendship," and "affection" are the kind which is meant. These activities are bound by specific norms in that it matters profoundly, according to the status of the other person in relation to the actor, what the latter does. He must be "loving," "friendly," "affectionate," as the case may be.

Finally, it is possible for expressional activities to be devoted to specific tasks for their own sake. A notable example is "disinterested" scientific research. The activity is bound by specific norms which vary according to its content. In the case of research, it is that of verifiable "truth." This is, perhaps, a borderline case in that the analysis of the motivation of such activities leads to understandable reasons why they are valued, involving their relation to the actor's general value-orientation, perhaps particularly to his religious attitudes. A notable case is the way in which the Calvinistic orientation placed a peculiar valuation on scientific work as a means of "knowing God through his works."[67]

---

67 See R. K. Merton, *Science, Technology and Society in Seventeenth Century England*, *Osiris*, 4: 360-632 (1938). This type of expressional activity particularly as exemplified in this kind of motivation of scientific research, is closely related to Max Weber's concept of *Wertrationalität*. The latter is, in the present terms, expressional, in that it is not primarily oriented to a goal, but to the "acting out" of a subjective attitude, relatively regardless of consequences. It differs from other expressional types (1) in that it emphasizes self-conscious rationality and (2) in that the empirical course of action acquires meaning by being the direct obedience to mandates of a subjective value system, rather than appropriate, but indirect, "symbolic" expression of it. The Crusades constitute, in part, a *wertrational* manifestation of medieval Catholicism, the Gothic cathedrals, in the same sense or degree, do not. On Weber's concept, see *Wirtschaft und Gesellschaft* (Tübingen: J.C.B. Mohr, 1925), especially Chapter I, Section 2, and *The Structure of Social Action*, (*op. cit.*), Chapter XVII.

Certain general remarks about expressional activities can be made. In the first place, this classification, more than the others, is not only significant as formulating types, but also elements which are often combined in varying ways in the same concrete case. The types thus "shade off" into one another almost imperceptibly. Secondly, symbolic relationships play a peculiarly significant role in the field of expressional activities. In one way or another the things done and the immediate goals will be found to be capable of analysis in terms of their "appropriateness" to what is expressed. They cannot, by definition, be significant as means to further ends.

Finally, these activities, like others, are "integrated" with the total action system of the individual, above all, with his major orientations. This is particularly important in understanding *what* is expressed. No fundamental attitude or orientation is likely to be altogether dissociated from the individual's principal expressional activities. Children, in their play, will often dramatize their family relationships. "Religious art" is precisely so important because religion is important in society. Its relative absence is prominent in times of "secularization." In their friendships and their love relationships, people will manifest the basic sentiments appropriate to their major orientations and will form expectations of the behavior of the other party in accordance with them. Indeed, expressional activities are not analytical elements of action, but concrete modes of action in which *all* the important elements are focused. In this respect they are similar to the other structuralized modes.

C. The Functional Differentiation of Social Systems

The same order of functional differentiation which has just been outlined for the case of the action system of the individual has its application to social systems as a whole. But before taking up the analogous classification as such, it is necessary to make a few remarks about the special complications which arise in this connection.

In the first place, it is not the individual "actor" as a unit which is the primary unit of reference in analyzing this mode of differentiation;

it is the "role." A role, it will be remembered, is a defined mode of activity which is differentiated from others. In his capacity of "member" of groups and "party" to social relationships, the individual actor plays a more or less well-defined role. Though, of course, he cannot in the strictest sense play more than one role at the same time, he alternates in the ordinary course of life between actions which are appropriate to the different roles in which he belongs. While in the "office," he is in the roles of "earner," "producer," "boss," and, when he comes home, he may switch to those of "husband" and "father." On Sunday, he may be "churchgoer," and so on. But it goes without saying that every role is the role *of* an individual actor, and this fact determines certain important conditions of the structure of roles. There is a limit to the capacity of any one actor to play, even at different times, altogether contradictory roles, and his action in the different roles is more or less integrated and in a state of mutual interdependence.

It is conceivable [68] that in a social system there should be no differentiation of roles at all, or at least no permanent differentiation. Age differentiation is an example which is not permanent. But this state would require the "abolition" of sex differentiation, and in all societies there is some differentiation of the roles of members of the sexes. [69] But there are certain roles, notably the most generalized in the kinship system, which, in the course of a normal lifetime, are played by all, or the great majority of the actors in a social system – in this case, notably, "child," "spouse," and "parent." In specific structures, others like "friend" or, in the Greek polis, "citizen" may not only be universalized, but have approximately the same content for all. But this is never strictly true of *all* the roles in a social system. There is a tendency to specialization of types, not in the sense that the individuals in question perform *only* the specialized role, which is at best a limiting case, but that they perform, among their various roles, certain ones which others either do not perform at all or perform only to a minor degree. Thus, almost every normal man is hus-

68 That is, "objectively possible" in Max Weber's sense.

69 On a social, not *only* a biological level.

band and father, but only a small proportion in our society are university professors.

The differentiation of roles has a very important implication. Precisely insofar as an individual devotes himself to specialized roles, he becomes dependent on others for functions which he is thereby excluded from performing himself, at all or in adequate degree. The beginning of this mutual interdependence through the differentiation of roles is to be found on a biological level, exemplified by the fact that "a man cannot have a baby." But in many social systems this "division of labor" becomes elaborated into a very complex structure.

The first striking feature of this structure is the fact that it lends every role to a greater or less degree a double aspect. The actor is, on the one hand, the "performer" of functions for the collectivity, and thus, in one way or another, for the other individuals in it (including those as yet unborn); on the other hand, he is the "receiver" of "services" and their material results, performed by other actors, including, of course, those long dead. In certain circumstances, there takes place the development of specific mechanisms by virtue of which these two aspects of differentiated roles are related. The most notable of these, perhaps, is money. In certain cases, then, there may be two aspects of the position or function of the individual, what he "does" or "puts into it" and what he "gets out of it," which, in case of pecuniary remuneration, is formally differentiated.

This double aspect of roles has a very important bearing on the problem of motivation. Since both aspects always concretely go together, it is often difficult to say what their relative parts are. Does a professor teach and write because he "likes his work" or "to promote the advancement of science" or because he "needs the money" or is "avaricious?" Neither is probably, in the usual case, an accurate diagnosis. Indeed, the interdependence of these things is so close that it is only by *comparative* analysis that the variables can be isolated and their relations established.

The "division of labor" makes it possible for the individual to devote himself, to an otherwise impossible degree, to specialized activities, particularly the less "utilitarian" ones, because the utilitarian functions, so far as they are important to him, are performed by others. And the others need not simply "sacrifice" themselves to do this, because on the receiving side of their roles they may be quite amply remunerated. Indeed, it often happens that the persons performing the less essential functions have the "harder" time of it.

When roles are thus differentiated, the performer of a specialized role always in some sense "needs" what he "gets out of it" in exchange. Then to some extent his activity in that role is goal-directed with the remuneration, whatever form it takes, as the goal. But whether in its functional aspect, it is also primarily goal-directed depends on the content of the activity. Even if it is, however, it is directed to other goals than that of remuneration – the making of goods, the solving of a scientific problem, the winning of a military campaign, etc. But even expressional activities, so far as they are engaged in specialized roles, become inevitably bound up with goal-direction, hence, in this as well as other senses, with the "self-interest" of the actor. The same is true of religious activities which, by definition, in their manifest functional aspect cannot be directed to any empirical goals. This fact is one of the fundamental bases of the continual tendency to "commercialization" of disinterested activity-patterns and the "secularization" of religion, and perhaps, still more, of the ideological significance of suspicion of such commercialization.

In view of these features, the functional specialization of social systems in terms of roles is more complex than that of the action-system of the individual. Every specialized role has its remunerative aspect. But apart from that, the basic starting point is, functionally, the same. Some of the specialized activities are significant as modes of achievement of the socially important goals, that is, those important to the collectivity treated as a unit, and those important to members of the collectivity other than the actor in question – usually both of these two aspects will be involved in concrete cases. Other roles will be primarily centered about the expressional type of activity, so far as its functional status in the social system is concerned, giving rise to such phenomena as the "artist," the "professional" athlete or player of games, and the like.

There seems to be a strong tendency, among the *specialized* roles played by a given individual, for one to become definitely dominant, and to be tied up with the actor's dominant remunerative interests. This may be called his "occupation." Hence, the dominant aspect of the "division of labor" of social systems, though by no means its only important aspect, tends to be the system of occupational roles. The organization of these roles takes place in terms of sub-systems grouped more or less definitely about the basic functional differentiation outlined in the last section.

In the first place, there is what may be called the "technological-economic" system. It is the system of organized and differentiated activities by which the means to empirical ends are made available and applied by rational procedures. Whether the end to which they are ultimately applied is transcendental or serving an expressional function does not matter in this connection; essentially the same analytical considerations apply, and they can all become the content of specialized occupations. This is as true of the "production" of the bread and wine used in the Eucharist, or of a sculptor's tools, as it is of agricultural implements. It is all part of the system of "production" of the society.

Every actor in the social system is in some degree related to the system of production in the role of "consumer" in either or both of two ways. On the one hand, he is dependent on that system for the meeting of what are usually thought of as his personal consumption needs, food, clothing, shelter, and the convenience of life. On the other hand, he is dependent on it, almost no matter what his role or occupation, for the "properties" of his occupational activity. This is true whether this activity is "part" of the system of production or not. A priest uses vestments, implements, and a church building which somebody has to produce. A symphony orchestra uses at the very least instruments, music, and a building, which again somebody has to produce. But, on the other or "functional" side, only part of the differentiated occupations are, in this sense, "productive," those whose *manifest* function is to contribute to this productive process.

The economic and the technological aspects of the productive system are closely interwoven. The principal aspects of this have already been discussed and need not be repeated. But there is, in this as in other respects, a tendency to the differentiation of roles. Some roles, like that of the industrial worker, may be primarily technological in their functional significance; others, like that of the modern business man, especially the merchant or banker, are more directly economic in significance.

Goal-directed activity in the action system of the individual was, so far as it was subject to the normative standard of empirical rationality, limited to the technological-economic type. Relations to other actors were involved but only in the role of technologically and economically significant means and conditions of the attainment of empirical ends. But, on the social level, there is the possibility for the control of the action of other individuals to become the primary manifest function of specialized roles, in particular, occupational roles. There seem to be two primary aspects of this, the "executive" function and the "political" function.

Much goal-directed activity depends for efficiency and economy on the coordinated activity of a plurality of individuals. In the simpler types of cooperation, it may be spontaneous and informal, but, in the more complex types, the function of coordination itself involves higher technical problems and becomes the central focus of specialized roles. This can happen where the content of the activity is oriented to any sort of goal whatever, economic production, military conquest or defense, attainment of political power, administration of a church or a scientific society. [70]

On the other hand, the possibility of mutual influence of individuals and of affective malintegration gives rise to the "problem of order." Again, in relatively simple systems, this may be "taken care of" entirely

---

70 For further discussion see below, pp. 157ff.

by informal mechanisms, such as, "custom," with its sanctions of disapproval and of informal self-appointed overt control and punishment. Probably the stability of every social system rests primarily on these informal mechanisms of social control. But in the more complex systems organized activity directed to this functional situation tends to develop. For the reasons already pointed out, the problem of order tends to focus above all on the spatial location of individuals, with its attendant consequences and susceptibility to physical coercion and compulsion by the use of force. Hence, there is a tendency for specialized roles to develop, or persons specifically "authorized," to maintain order and coordinate activities of significance to the collectivity as a unit within a territorial area and by means, at least as a last resort, of physical force. It is, perhaps, a variant of the "executive" function, but one which has such specific characteristics as to justify its differentiation as "political."

All action in social systems is, as has been shown, subject to normative control. Some implications of this fact will be taken up later. But the functionally differentiated "political" roles have a peculiar relation to the normative patterns of the social group. From the functional point of view, the primary "justification" of such roles, and of the attendant power and authority, must be the "enforcement" of the recognized normative patterns. But, on the other hand, the strain put on the performance of a functionally defined role by the involvement of differentiated roles with the elements of "self-interest," particularly as those come in through the "division of labor," is perhaps greater in this field than any other, not excepting that of economic production. There seem to be two primary reasons for this. On the one hand, political authority, like other functions, requires for its efficient exercise the effective control over the technologically requisite means. But in this case the means are particularly potent and hence subject to abuse. Power, in a broad sense, and particularly physical force, are dangerous weapons. Secondly, for a variety of reasons, but almost universally, positions of political authority have come to carry with them a very high level of prestige in social groups. Hence the interest in recognition is very powerful in this field, and less directly, other related interests in response, in pecuniary rewards, etc. Indeed, in one main aspect, the political system is at the same time the "apex" of the system of social integration and the most precarious in its stability.

It is possible for the goal-directed activities of individuals to be oriented to other normative standards than the empirically rational means-end relationship. Such activities may also become the focus of specialized roles. Indeed, in the ritual field, they are one of the most prominent types in relatively simple societies. Hence, there may be various types of magician, notably weather-magic in its relations to crops and health magic. Often there is a specialization, so that, in the same primitive society, there are several types of magic, each carried out by a different person on behalf of the whole group.

This mode of specialization calls attention to an important structural principle. It may be said that the primary basis of the differentiation of roles, as of activity systems, is the division of the principal functional modes of orientation. And this is, indeed, the main principle on which the different main "role-structures" are differentiated from each other. But, within those role-structures and to some degree cutting across them, there is an important basis of differentiation in terms of the similarity of means to many different ends. That is, several ends may all employ the same means and the person specialized in the use of the means may employ them for all the ends. Thus the differentiation of the content of roles forms a kind of criss-cross pattern, repeated on a variety of different levels.

The non-empirical teleological orientation also becomes the focus of a very important class of roles, notably, the religious. Religious, like technological, action is something participated in by virtually all members of a given social system, but it is possible for given individuals to become specialized in religious orientation and functions. There seem to be two principal modes of this.

Every stable and established social structure is characterized by a more or less well-defined and well-integrated "religion," which is relatively speaking shared by all the members of the group. Every individual as part of this integrated group activity participates in "religious action." But such a sub-system of a social system of action is not undifferentiated. Within it there develop specialized roles which, in some cases, come to take on occupational status. The most "primitive" and universal type of this is the kind of role concerned with administration of the "cult" of a religion, that is, of its ritual. Very generally ritual becomes the object of technical specialization, a more or less esoteric mystery.

The other basis of specialization lies in the fact that such a sub-system of action, like others, is not left to "informal" modes of cooperation, but becomes "organized." This means a differentiation of authority and the development of roles concerned with the executive function – the making of decisions important to the group, the administration of discipline, group finances, relations to other groups, and so forth. The most striking example of development of group organization and the attendant executive roles in a religious group is, of course, the Roman Catholic Church.

The above types of roles are concerned with functions on behalf of the religious orientation of the group as a whole. It can safely be said that no large-scale total society has, as a whole, ever been overwhelmingly devoted to the "religious life" as such. It has, however, been quite common for considerable numbers of individuals to be so devoted. In a sense, such individuals, notably, "monks" and "nuns," perform a specialized role. Its functional relation to the whole social group, if any, may be said to be secondary. They do, however, occupy a differentiated status, the relation of which to the general occupational structure raises peculiar and often crucial problems.

In general terms the modes of social structuralization of expressional activities are similar to the goal-directed ones. Any one of these may become the dominant content of occupational roles. The individual then becomes a "professional" in the playing of games, in art, or in scientific research. The only one of the four dominant expressional types which seems not to lend itself to this kind of development is the primarily affective expression of attitudes toward persons. It seems to be necessary for such activities to have an impersonal object in order for them to become the content of occupational roles.

One crucially important effect of the professionalization of expressional activities is an immense heightening of the significance of the normative aspect of the activity and a corresponding weakening of its character as "free" expression. The essential basis of this lies in the fact that the "professional" plays or produces or performs for an audience or a public, not for his own private "amusement" or edification alone. He necessarily becomes oriented to the goal of "success" in a much higher degree. He will also be subject to invidious comparison with other professionals in a sense in which this is seldom true of the "amateur."

On the side of the public, the working of this structure is primarily manifested in a set of "expectations" in terms of which the performance of the professional is measured. One significant aspect of this lies in the fact that for many or most of the audience, their passive, vicarious reception of the performer's expression is a kind of substitute for their own free and independent expression.

On the side of the professional himself, there is, on the one hand, a heightened "seriousness" in his devotion to the role. What is to the amateur a free time activity or at most an "avocation" becomes to the professional the object of his "career." At the same time, this means a different order of integration with his "self-interest." Success and failure mean all that occupational achievement in any field means. This may, in one respect, be an important source of the very high levels of achievement in these fields sometimes found in highly differentiated societies, particularly in the linking of an expressional content common to a society with very high levels of technical skill, as in literary or musical composition and performance.

But, given imperfect integration, this may also be one of the primary sources of the "degradation" and "perversion" of expressional forms and standards. For though "integration" calls for a fusion of self-interested elements of motivation with "disinterested" devotion to realization of a normative pattern in the highest degree, through various relatively well-known mechanisms, this fusion can be broken down at the expense of the normative standards. "Commercialization" and other forms of disruptive tendencies are as fundamental here as in political or economic activity. The basis problems and mechanisms of social control are much the same in all fields.

Expressional activities, like others, may or may not be carried on in organized form. Where they are, there is a secondary differentiation of roles in that persons may become specialized in the executive aspect of them. Such functions as that of the orchestra conductor or the director of a theatrical production belong in this class.

Expressional activities are like religious ones in that they are, as the content of specialized roles, by no means always carried out "on behalf of" the social group as a whole. Individualistic tendencies of devotion to "art" relatively regardless of its significance to common values are especially important here. There is often a subtle transition between these two main phases of peculiar devotion to expressional activities, as to religion. As in the latter case, there is always the possibility of "conversion" of a public to the "cult" of a creative artist.

Finally, a few words need to be said about an important mode of interrelation between goal-directed and expressional activities, apart from the fact that they both share the same basic orientations of the actors in a social system and, in a sense, are "manifestations" of them.

According to the interpretation put forward in this essay, action in pursuit of a particular goal is never, as it were, "self-sufficient," but always takes place within a kind of "matrix" of organized and integrated settled modes of orientation. These are variously called "persistent aggregates," "conditioned reflexes," "attitude sets," and even, erroneously, "instincts." One very important criterion of the "rationality" of a course of action is the degree and extensity of "emancipation" from the underlying personality structure or orientation.

On the whole, the greater the degree of rational emancipation from the orientation matrix, the more definitely is a course of activity "goal-directed;" while the more definitely embedded in the orientation matrix it is, the more, as a totality, it tends to be expressional. In every actual large-scale system of what is treated as goal-directed activity this underlying expressional aspect is of prime importance. It tends to become of increasing importance as either of two antitheses to the pole of rational action is approached.

Following Max Weber[71] these may be spoken of as traditional and affectual action respectively. In the one case, the range of considerations open to rational consideration is narrowly limited by certain fixed factors. These are "taken for granted," that is, they are so deeply embedded in the structure of personality that their "advisability" is not even considered. Such fixity is, moreover, not confined to random individuals, but constitutes a uniformity on the social level.[72] Affectual action is, for Weber, simply a name for nontraditional modes of orientation which are yet not rationally oriented to specific goals.

---

[71] *Wirtschaft und Gesellschaft, op. cit.*, Chapter I, Section 2.

[72] Such a uniformity is not, of course, analytically ultimate. The traditionalism of patterns is a mode of "structuralization" of action.

VII. Institutions, "Formal Organization" and Law

This outline would be seriously incomplete if it entirely omitted consideration of certain general aspects of the structuralization of social systems which cut across the functional differentiation both of types of activity and of roles. The problem of order, and hence the role of social control, has formed one of the central themes of the whole treatment of social systems. It has also been seen that a functionally adequate "solution" of the problem of order involves the subjection of action to rules which enjoin certain types of action, prohibit others, and which generally define the limits of permissible action in various directions, including both goals to be pursued and choice of means. These rules, of course, constitute part of the normative patterns governing action.

A. Institutions

Among the many different classes and types of rules governing action, there is one which needs to be singled out because of its special functional significance to social systems. Unfortunately, it cannot be defined in very simple terms. Rules of this type will be called "institutions."

The first criterion is the definition of socially important patterns – notably, regulating the status [73] of individuals and the "forms" of social relationships. Put somewhat differently, they are the normative patterns defining the "legitimate expectations" of others with respect to the action of the individual in question. This leads over into another phase of the problem which will be taken up presently.

The second criterion is the attachment of moral sanctions to such patterns. When a rule occupies institutional status in a social system, there is a *moral* obligation to conform with it. Deviant behavior typically arouses the reaction, on the part of others, of moral indignation.

---

[73] See above, pp. 127ff.

Insofar as the social system is "institutionally" integrated, the correlative of moral indignation is the feeling of guilt on the part of the actor himself.

But not every norm which on the part of some actor or actors is considered a subject of moral obligation is institutional in character. The third criterion is that the pattern has, in a particular sense, become part of the "social structure." What is perhaps the key to this phase of the problem lies in the significance of the term "expectations." In a society like that of the present, a few individuals may, with intense moral fervor, feel an obligation to devote themselves with great energy to religiously ascetic practices. It can hardly, however, be said that the majority in the social system legitimately expect any one to act in this way. Such a pattern is, in this society, clearly in a different status from the expectation that a man will, for instance, care adequately for his immature children, or work faithfully and efficiently at his job.

What distinguishes institutional from non-institutional moral obligations would appear to be mainly three things. In the first place, there is the extensity of the area of recognition of moral obligation. For any given social system, only those are institutional obligations which are relatively *generally* recognized. "Private" moral obligations, or those only recognized by special limited groups, on the other hand, are not institutional in the wider social system.

There are two important conditions to observe in interpreting this proposition. What constitutes a "social system" is, in a certain sense, relative. Institutional patterns, by no means in any given concrete case, all refer to the same circle of actors. Monogamy in the Western world is a pattern with a much broader area of recognition than is primogeniture in its relation to the British aristocracy. But both are unquestionably institutional. Furthermore, there are differences in the degree, within a given circle, of integration with an institutional pattern. Within the group of those to whom the pattern is supposed or expected to apply, there are wide variations in the actual effectiveness of its recognition. But making allowance for these facts, the moral values sanctioning an institutional pattern are always *common* values. Institutions are "manifestations" of a common value system.

The second condition touches the fact that common values and moral attitudes do not necessarily impose the *same* obligations on all individuals who recognize them. This follows from the fact of differentiation of status and role. One of the simplest cases is that of the differentiation of sex role. Men and women, over a considerable area, are expected to do different things, but the values and corresponding moral sentiments are common to both sexes. Men's expectations as to the proper behavior for women are often just as important in determining what a woman shall do as are those of other women and vice versa.

But this "extensity" of sharing of the common values sanctioning a system of institutional rules is only one "dimension" of their institutional status. There is, in addition, an "intensive" dimension. This is perhaps indicated by a term often linked with institutions – the statement that they are "established." Here again the implications of the term expectations form a valuable starting point. Other individuals are expected to conform to an institutional norm not only in the sense that an actor *approves* conformity or *hopes* they will conform, but that it is something on which he can count and he feels entitled to be indignant if he is disappointed. This must mean that persons in the relevant status and role normally *do* conform with a relatively high degree of approximation. The norms which are institutionally established are not "utopian." An example is the rule that a man shall be married to only one wife at a time. There are many other respects in which the norms governing the marriage relation are widely violated. But bigamy is so infrequent that, from a structural point of view, it may be regarded as quite negligible. In the degree to which a normative pattern is institutionalized, it tends to be "taken for granted" and the question whether or not it should be violated is not even raised for the average individual acting in relation to it.

This means that most others who are personally involved in the relevant situation expect it to be conformed with and are indignant and "let down" if it is not. On the other hand, the actor himself has it built into the structure of his own personality. Hence action in relation to it is, as has been seen throughout, not in the usual sense purely "ethical" or disinterested, but the actor's own interests have become bound up with it. This is true, on the one hand, because the satisfaction of these interests is, in the various ways noted above, bound up with the actions and attitudes of the persons who expect him to conform. On the other hand, his own self-respect and "peace of mind," in a word his personal equilibrium, is dependent on avoiding the internal conflicts which violation on a considerable scale would bring.

The implications of the institutionalization of normative patterns can be brought out in a slightly different way. W. I. Thomas classifies the elements involved in action as, on the one hand, the subjective "wishes" of the actor, on the other hand, the "definition of the situation." What have been referred to as purely "ethical" norms belong definitely in the subjective category. The situation is significant only with respect to its relative favorableness or unfavorableness to their realization. But, insofar as norms become institutionally established, they become part of the definition of the situation. They shall retain their "ideal" or normative character, but there is, in their significance to action, something more than this. On the one hand, violation entails objective consequences – the disapproval, hatred, or obstruction of other important individuals and the effect on the actor's own personality. On the other hand, the very fact that the actor himself and other actors accept such norms "defines" the situation in another sense. It defines the perspective in which the situation is seen, what aspects of it are important and what are not. In short, it is a large part of the structure by virtue of which the situation takes on meaning.

The relation of institutions to cognitive orientation is relatively complex. It has already been said that the more completely institutionalized a norm is, the more its obligatoriness tends to be "taken for granted." The same is likely to be true of its cognitive justification, which is seldom explicitly self-conscious for those accepting its institutional authority.

This fact is connected with the tendency for explicit cognitive formulations to be oriented to critically problematical subject matters. Hence the explicit formulation of the problem of meaning and of proposed "solutions" need to be treated with special caution. They are always articulated with the accepted institutional system, but not necessarily directly *its* primary cognitive rationalization.

B. "Formal Organization"

It has already been pointed out that action in social systems is subject to control in terms of normative patterns in informal ways. In some societies and groups, almost all normative patterns, including the most important institutions, are entirely informally enforced. In all societies this is true of a large proportion, and the same mechanisms also underlie formal enforcement where this is present. Nevertheless, the phenomenon of formal organization is one of the crucial phenomena of social structure in the enforcement of conformity with normative patterns and in the coordination of the actions of a plurality of individual actors.

There seem to be three main aspects of "formal organization" – its bearing on the constitution of groups, on the exercise of and subjection to authority, and, finally, on the *relation* of the individual actor to normative patterns.

The concept "group" is in the first instance simply a matter of naming one of the primary consequences of the fact that social systems are differentiated. The different actors and their activities are not differentiated at random, but form definite sub-patterns of social structure. As long as the actor is taken as the unit of a patterned aggregate that is less extensive than the whole social system, this aggregate is a "group."

There seem to be two main types of groups. They may be called the "statistical" group and the "interaction" group. The former consists merely of persons to whom common criteria apply, whatever they may be and regardless of any empirical interrelations. Thus all women, all cases of tuberculosis, or all subscribers to the *New York Times* constitute such groups. They are of no further interest in the present connection.

The members of an interaction group, on the other hand, are related by direct ties of mutual interdependence, so that if any one is changed in his characteristics or actions, this produces changes in the others. It goes without saying that groups in this sense are formed wherever there is a structure of activities in social systems. Also, whether they are formally organized or not, groups vary greatly in the definiteness and importance of "membership" in them. It should always be borne in mind that the individual actor participates in a given group, not as a whole, but only in one "sector" of his total personality.

A group in this sense always has a certain "life" of its own. It takes a more or less definite place in the broader social system, performs "functions" within it, seeks, as a unit, goals within it, and tends more or less to influence the direction of change of the broader system. It also faces a problem of internal "control," of coordinating the activities of its members in conformity with the needs of its unitary action in the larger social system, notably in relation to other groups, and enforcing conformity with the normative patterns which constitute one of the basic foci of group unity.[74]

Such groups are only in an empirically negligible limiting case entirely undifferentiated internally. The larger social systems to which they fit may be differentiated in a number of respects, as, for instance, by technological differentiation of roles. There is, however, one plane of differentiation which is of primary significance in the present connection. The relation of a group to the external situation, including, of course, the *social* situation, is complex and continually changing. These changes have complex repercussions on internal relations within the group. There is, hence, a strong tendency for the adjustment of these changing relations to become a specialized function within the group, that of "leadership."[75] This, insofar as it becomes the content of definite

[74] See Chester I. Barnard, *Dilemmas of Leadership in the Democratic Process* (Princeton: Princeton University Press, 1939) and, more generally, his *The Functions of the Executive* (Cambridge: Harvard University Press, 1938).

[75] This is not a very suitable term, but seems to be the best available. It is here used in the most general sense.

roles, in turn involves authority over the members. If the leader (or organized body of such) is to be in a position to adjust the group as a whole, he must be in a position to influence the action of its members, in order effectively to carry out his plans or policies.

The differentiation of the leadership sub-group from those who are led in a group has a double implication for the status of the normative patterns governing the action of the members. On the one hand, there is a new content for these patterns – the definition of the status and role of those in positions of leadership, which includes the extent of their authority and its limits in the "rights" of the members. Only so far as normative patterns are extended to include this is the position and content of leadership and control "legitimate." On the other hand, the necessity for authority and control of leadership to be effective means partly that a main object of normative patterns is to secure the authority of the leadership for group functions, partly that the authority of leadership tends to be fused with the authority to *enforce* whatever normative patterns are recognized in the group as binding, particularly as institutionally established. The two functions, that of leadership and of the enforcement of normative patterns within the group, are analytically distinct, but they are so closely related that it is almost unknown for them to be completely separated in concrete structuralization. The "executive" or "governmental" authority almost invariably participates in both functions.

The basic phenomenon under consideration is the development of a specialized status, with the corresponding roles, of authority within groups, that of leadership or "government." This functionally basic status may, of course, be subject to further differentiation in various ways. Perhaps the most important sub-classification is that involved in the "classical" theory of the "separation of powers," that into "executive," "legislative," and "judicial" functions. This further differentiation is, however, of secondary importance for present purposes.

It should go without saying that such a fundamentally important type of status must be more or less well integrated with the rest of the system. In the first place, the limits of authority and rights in different groups must be more or less well coordinated so that group rivalries and conflicts are not too disruptive, either on the macroscopic level, as in the conflict of Church and State, or within the individual personality in the form of acutely conflicting loyalties and obligations to two or more groups. This, of course, leads into one main aspect of the problems of "political pluralism." The functional need for this type of integration is one of the main reasons for the importance of the "state," along with the functional importance of order on a territorial basis, and of physical coercion and compulsion. Perhaps, indeed, it is the need for this integration which largely explains the fact that, so persistently, the political functions in the narrower sense, and that of coordination of the total group structure of a society tend to come under the control of the same concrete system of formal organization, hence, of the same "authorities."

But the functional need of integration does not apply to group structures, as such, alone. It is also essential that, to a considerable degree, these statuses in the group structures should be integrated with the scale of stratification. The functions of exercising authority and the incumbents of the corresponding positions need to be valued. It seems a safe generalization that everywhere authority forms one of the basic criteria of high status, which, of course, works both ways. Persons in authority are ranked high by virtue of this fact and, vice versa, persons enjoying high rank on other grounds tend to acquire positions of authority.

The relative universality of the high valuation of authority is founded in the structure of social systems of action in a way somewhat similar to that in which the relative universality of the valuation of wealth is founded. In both cases, they can, within certain limits, be abstracted from the particular content of the role or status – its functions in the case of authority, the detailed content of the things possessed in the case of wealth. Within limits the wealthy man is the man well supplied with the possessions which are valued in his society, whatever they may be. Yams, which are highly prized in the Trobriands, would be little valued in modern America, while pearls are little valued in the Trobriands. This abstraction, in the case of wealth, is pushed to a still higher degree by the device of money, so that what a man has is less possessions than a blank check to secure whatever possessions he may want – again within limits.

In the sphere of authority, the integration of the system of formal organization of the society in something like the "state" plays a role somewhat akin to that of money in the economic context. There is such a thing as "supreme authority" and highly generalized authority, culminating in the theory of "absolutism" and "dictatorship." But even apart from that authority is generalized – it is the legitimized power to get other people to do the things which it is considered important that they should do. Hence, apart from certain peculiar value orientations where authority as such is suspect, corresponding to certain religious objections to wealth as such, authority will tend to be universally valued and its holders to occupy a high status. This is, of course, by no means to say that there are not qualitative differentiations according to the content of authority as, apart from complete "monetization," there always are with regard to wealth. It is not a matter either of the number of persons over whom authority is held, or of the "intensity" of that authority, as such and alone.

The parallel to wealth can be carried a step farther. Persons in authority do not in any simple sense merely carry out the "corporate will" of groups. There is also an important extent to which they "use" the groups over which they have authority and control to realize their own goals. There is, in general, a complex balance between these two aspects of the relation of group and leader, sometimes leaning more in one direction, sometimes in the other. There are, however, many individual goals which cannot be carried out without extensive authority over other persons, as there are many goals which require a large expenditure of economic "means."

Furthermore, just as wealth can, because of instrumental use of its symbolic value, and the prestige of its possession, become an immediate goal, so can authority. There is then, apart from the primary functional role of authority in formal organization, necessarily a secondary significance of authority as a goal of ambition, because it carries prestige and power to attain whatever goals the individual may cherish. The inevitable result is a struggle of individuals for the occupation of positions of institutionalized power, of authority, which cannot be altogether eliminated, and can only be regulated with difficulty. Institutions, thus, must not only regulate the role of the person in power, define the scope of his authority and its limits in the rights of others, but they must regulate the paths by which persons attain and are excluded from positions of authority. The strains involved in this structural situation are well known to be one of the most prolific sources of social instability.

Authority is, it has been said, apart from certain special cases, universally valued. But it is not by any means necessarily in an unequivocal position in the value orientation of a social system. In the first place, the valuation of a given individual incumbent, of the person in a position of authority, will depend not only on the fact that he has the position, but to a greater or less degree on how he acts in it, whether his goals are approved, and whether he adheres to the institutional definitions of his role. There is an opening for much strain here. But, secondly, authority must compete, in the scale of valuation, with many other things, including, notably, wealth apart from authority, birth, and personal qualities and achievements other than those of which the attainment of positions of authority can be regarded as a direct index. Some of these are closely related to authority, others are specifically foreign to it, and can easily come into conflict with the claims of authority for recognition. [76]

The exact problem of integration will vary with the content of the relevant value orientation in the given case, but very generally a point of

---

[76] One of the most interesting cases of this is to be found in the role of technical competence and achievement as involved in the development of science and the professions in our society. In these fields, the basis of ranking in order of eminence is quite distinct from any relations of authority or subordination. The most brilliant scientist may be deplorably tyrannized over by his secretary. But in a social structure where authority plays a very prominent role, it is easy for its patterns of valuation to invade these other fields.

serious strain is to be found in the relations of authority to other bases of eminence in the scale of stratification. This difficulty is complicated by the fact that the person in authority generally has coercive sanctions at his disposal, as well as propaganda resources and the like. Hence, when there is a strain or when any shift in relative valuation occurs which is unfavorable to the status of authority, there is always the possibility that it will be met with repressive measures which seek to restore the status quo or go beyond it. This is one aspect of the phenomena of "totalitarianism." The fact, however, that non-authoritarian positions and achievements have, by and large, enjoyed such a large measure of prestige in history attests to the limits both of the exercise of naked power, and to the limits imposed on authority by institutional patterns of "legitimacy."

C. Law

It has already been pointed out that the development of formal organization introduces an important complication into the system of normative patterns and their relation to the action of individuals. In explaining adherence or deviation, we may speak of three levels of the problem of "enforcement." First is the purely "subjective" motivational complex of the actor, regardless of any possible "external" consequences. Second are those external consequences which arise from the "spontaneous" unorganized reaction of others to his action, disapproval, withdrawal of hedonic benefits, ostracism, etc. with their antitheses on the positive side. It should be clear that all of these may have either an intrinsic or a symbolic significance or both. No set of normative patterns can be said to be "institutionalized" unless this second order of considerations is prominently developed. And, third, with formal organization another level enters in. Normative patterns become the special concern of a functionally differentiated group, those exercising governing authority in the group. They carry on the functions of promulgating, interpreting, and executing the patterns, with the authority to apply sanctions in case of recalcitrance. It is insofar as their administration has come to be the specialized function of such a differentiated governing authority with power to apply sanctions that the term "law" will be applied to normative patterns governing action.[77]

The development of formal organization is not only a crucially significant phenomenon of social systems because it opens up new possibilities of the coordination and direction of human activities, or because it opens up new sources of instability in the struggle for positions of power and authority with the attendant possibilities of twisting the use of power away from the institutionally sanctioned patterns. Its significance, further, does not, in addition to the above points, lie only in the additional strength lent to the enforcement system by the systematic application of sanctions.

The fact that certain normative patterns become the specialized object of attention of a functionally specialized group, leads to a certain kind of "official" interpretation of normative patterns and of the sanctions applied for nonconformity with them. Since, in every system of authority, there is some element of "executive discretion" this "official" specification of the pattern is to some degree always extended to the power to "make" rules, even though almost without exception with some restrictions of a procedural nature. There are a large number of reasons why the official decisions with respect to what is the law cannot be wholly random and arbitrary in the *ad hoc* instance. There is a strong tendency to some kind of consistency either with tradition or with abstract principle of some kind. This tendency is, in the most general sense, explained by the functional necessity for the integration of social systems and their institutional patterns.

Some kind of official specification of the normative pattern is inherent in the very existence of governing authority in formally organized groups. But the extent to which this is formally rationalized to constitute a coherent system is highly variable. Any such tendencies may be inhibited at quite primitive stages by a variety of factors. There is, however, the possibility that under favorable conditions it will go a long way.

---

[77] This is the concept of law (*Recht*) employed, in a sociological context, by Max Weber. See *Wirtschaft und Gesellschaft* (*op. cit.*), Chapter I, Section 10.

This is usually true only when there is a certain differentiation between direct governing authority and authoritative opinion as to the *content* of the law. Even though final interpretations may rest with a monarch or a legislative body, the basic tradition of the law as a *system* of norms tends to be born mainly by a functionally specialized group. Insofar as these become differentiated out from other functions, the main focus of their role becomes their technical expertness as "learned" in the law, as "lawyers." It is a striking historical fact that very frequently the classes who developed a technical expertise of this sort the farthest have, as a group, stood outside the main formal organization of government of their groups, though often some of their members have held office. This is true of the Roman *jurisconsults*, the English bar, the Canon lawyers of the Church, the Confucian scholars who were expert in the "proprieties," the Indian Brahman priests in their legal capacity, and the Talmudic scholars of Judaism. Often, though the members of such classes have not, as such, had official status, their works, and the patterns they developed, have exercised a crucially important influence on the development of social structures and the underlying modes of orientation.

It should be clear that the term law, as used here, is not restricted to the "law of the state" but is applicable to the normative patterns, or the "order," which is treated as binding for the action of the members of any formally organized group. The larger the scale and the importance of the group, however, and the more stable its fundamental forms, the more likely it has been that it would develop a highly systematized body of law, and that its tradition would be in the hands of a specialized class of experts. In the Western world, of course, it is the state and the church which have undergone these developments in a pre-eminent degree.

VIII. Conclusion

It should hardly need to be pointed out that the above essay can only in a highly tentative sense claim to contain a complete "system" of the theory of action. In the first place, it, like its predecessor, is primarily concerned with the *structure* of empirical systems rather than with variables and analytical uniformities in a strict and systematic sense. The procedure has been to start with the most general aspects of the frame of reference, and to proceed from there to outlining the structure of systems on the most general and abstract level. Gradually as the systematic picture has been developed, a closer and closer approach has been made to the description of what constitutes "social structure" on the level of concreteness which is usually expected by the common sense of the social sciences. In this respect, what has been achieved is only the broadest sort of outline, a rapid sketch of such basic structural features as stratification, authority and rights, differentiation of roles, institutions, formal organization, and law. In such a development, there is no logical stopping place. Doubtless there are other structural aspects of equal or almost equal generality which have not been taken up. The object has been only to carry the analysis far enough to establish the links between the most general conceptual scheme and more familiar categories in common use. The fact that some edges are left without being neatly trimmed is of secondary importance. The really important thing is proof of the applicability of the generalized scheme to the clarification and systematization of thought about significant concrete empirical problems.

Index

A

B

C